# THE GREAT COOKS' GUIDE TO

**Woks,**
**Steamers & Fire Pots**

America's leading food authorities share their home-tested
recipes and expertise on cooking equipment and techniques

THE GREAT COOKS' GUIDE TO

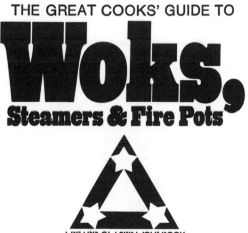

**Woks,**

**Steamers & Fire Pots**

A BEARD GLASER WOLF BOOK

RANDOM HOUSE, NEW YORK

Book Design by Milton Glaser, Inc.

Cover Photograph by Richard Jeffery

Library of Congress Cataloguing in Publication Data

The Great cooks' guide to woks, steamers & fire pots.
(The Great cooks' library)
1. Frying. 2. Steaming (Cookery) 3. Barbecue
cookery. 4. Kitchen utensils. I. Title: Woks,
steamers & fire pots. II. Series.
TX689.G73      641.5′8      77-5975
ISBN: 394-73425-4

Manufactured in the United States of America
8 9

We have gathered together some of the great cooks in this country to share their recipes—and their expertise—with you. As you read the recipes, you will find that in certain cases techniques will vary. This is as it should be: cooking is a highly individual art, and our experts have arrived at their own personal methods through years of experience in the kitchen.

**THE EDITORS**

# Contents

## WOK RECIPES

# STEAMER RECIPES

# FIRE POT RECIPES

# Woks, Steamers & Fire Pots

Think about it: you rarely see a fat Chinese person. Not because the Chinese don't enjoy eating; they certainly do, and they have developed a cuisine as subtle and refined as the French. They stay slim because the Chinese diet is generally low in starch and fats. They have found that texture, variety, and contrast of flavors please the palate far more than sheer abundance. For diet-conscious Westerners, the Chinese way of cooking lets us have our cake (or rather our shrimp with snow pea pods and mushrooms) and eat it too!

This healthful and delicious cuisine came about for a number of historical reasons. There are more Chinese on earth than any other ethnic group, yet only ten percent of their vast land is arable, so food is limited. Added to that, China has always suffered from a desperate lack of fuel. But whatever else they lack, the Chinese are rich in imagination. Centuries ago their ingenious response to scarcity was to evolve a method of cooking that made any bit of available food palatable while using the least possible amount of fuel. And so was born the wok, which means, simply, "cooking vessel." Made of thin metal and shaped like a salad bowl with handles, it fits perfectly into the round opening in the top of the traditional Chinese brazier. Fuel—kindling, bits of wood, charcoal and even straw—is fed to the stove through a front opening. Flames leap up to touch the thin metal bottom, diffusing heat through the wok. Oil—only a little—is added and rapidly heated; next comes the food, cut in uniform bits. The food is turned and tossed rapidly against the bottom and flaring sides of the wok, only long enough to sear the cut surfaces. The combination of oil and intense heat allows the small morsels to cook through before their cellular structure breaks down enough for them to release their juices. Flavor and goodness are sealed in.

**Stir-frying:** We call this method of cooking stir-frying, although scooping-tossing-searing describes it more closely. Every surface of each morsel gets equal time against the heated wok; no surface stays in place long enough to stick and thus begin to steam. One writer calls stir-frying a way to "surprise" food—he claims it's cooked before it even has time to know it's in the wok. Cantonese cooks use both ladle and spatula to stir-fry, agitating the food in a manner akin to tossing a salad at breakneck speed. Others use only one spatula, its base curved to conform to the flared shape of a wok. Grasping a wok handle with one hand to steady the pot,

**Classic Iron Wok & Ring Stand.** No pan is more versatile than the wok, used for stir-frying, braising, steaming and deep-frying. A diameter of 12″ or 14″ is recommended for best all-round use. A perforated ring stand stabilizes the round-bottomed wok.

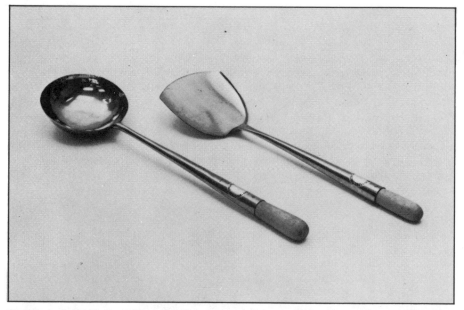

**Stainless-Steel Ladle & Spatula.** These rust-proof utensils are the essential tools of the wok trade. The spatula is curved to fit the slope of a wok's sides, and is especially useful in stir-frying. The ladle is used for both cooking and serving.

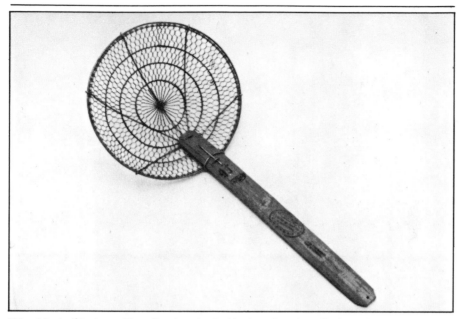

**Wire-Mesh Strainer.** The flat bowl of this bamboo-handled strainer is perfectly designed for scooping deep-fried foods out of the circle of oil in a wok.

they work the spatula held in the other hand around the circumference of the wok, scooping from the center to fling the bits of food against the far side. In either case, constant agitation is the key. It's a noisy process, and an exciting one: food hisses and sizzles as it makes contact with the hot oil, colors intensify in seconds, as bits of green pepper turn to glistening emerald, carrots glow like flame and cabbage quickens to a delicate jade. When you cook in a wok you substitute *your* energy for thermal energy. You plan ahead, slicing and chopping and arranging the food carefully, preparing it for the short time it will be in the pot.

For stir-frying, the foods to be cooked together are cut into uniform size. You won't need to acquire special skills for this; all cooking demands slicing, dicing, mincing or chopping. Chinese cooking just makes you more aware of it! In principal, you should be able to pick up any bit of food—ribbons of chicken, sections of asparagus, crunchy slices of water-chestnuts—with chopsticks. Even if you use a fork, just keep the chopstick image in mind when you slice, and you'll achieve the proper size and shape. Because chopping is so important to stir-frying, a good cutting tool is of great importance. A Chinese cleaver looks menacing, but its size

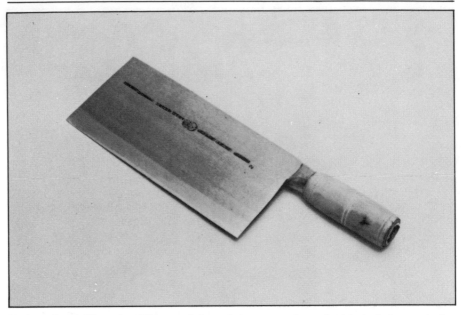

**Carbon Steel Chopping Cleaver.** A broad, heavy, rectangular-bladed cleaver is the best for all-purpose use: chopping, slicing, shredding and mincing. And tempered carbon-steel is preferred for its fine cutting edge. But keep it dry to prevent rust.

**Carbon-Steel Slicing Cleaver.** Although one good cleaver can fulfill most cutting needs, some cleavers are shaped to suit particular jobs. A slicing cleaver has a relatively narrow blade, lighter than the blade required for chopping, and the cutting edge is always straight.

**Hard Rock Maple Chopping Block**. To handle the myriad chopping, slicing and dicing chores in wok cookery, a professional-quality chopping block like this one is essential. In addition, a built-in knife sharpener will make it easier to keep your blades finely honed.

and weight actually speed up chopping and slicing once you get the hang of it. However, a good chef's knife works very well; just make sure it's *sharp*. (Incidentally, you're much more likely to cut yourself with a dull knife than a sharp one; a dull blade can glance off a bit of food and nick you sharply in the knuckles.) If you have a food processor and are not cooking traditional Chinese food, you can prepare stir-fry vegetables in a trice.

**Ingredients:** If you have access to Oriental vegetable and grocery shops, so much the better, but almost any of the meat and vegetables we ordinarily eat take readily to stir-frying if properly prepared. You don't have to "cook Chinese" to use the wok. For example, strips of veal with mushrooms, cognac and heavy cream is a traditional Swiss dish that adapts perfectly to wok cookery. And in this case, stir-frying is an improvement on pan-frying. In the wok the veal ribbons are sealed before they have a chance to steam, and the mushrooms retain a pristine crispness.

**Procedure:** With your chopped ingredients lined up and ready, turn on the

**Steel Wok with Handle**. For greater ease in handling, woks in different dimensions are available with a wooden handle and ring for hanging. A perforated ring stand is required with this round-bottomed pan to hold it stable on a Western stove.

heat and heat the wok for a minute or two, then ring the top of the wok with oil; it will heat as it drips down the sides. To test to see if the oil is the proper temperature, place a bit of food in it. The food should pop and sizzle noisily. Cook each recipe according to directions, but remember, you cannot double the amount of food cooked at one time with success. If you like, make two batches of a dish—not many stir-fry recipes take more than five minutes to cook. And no more than one pound of meat should be cooked at one time.

**Choosing a Wok:** The best are made of iron or carbon steel, though you have the choice of woks in stainless steel or aluminum as well. Both iron and steel need seasoning before being used for the first time. To season, scrub the wok well with detergent in hot water to remove its moisture-resistant film. Dry it, set it over medium heat, and rub the surface with paper toweling soaked in vegetable oil. After three minutes, rub off the oil with clean toweling, and re-oil the wok. (Leave the wok on the heat throughout the seasoning process.) Rub it clean and oil it two more times; the wok is now ready for use. To clean a wok, use only hot water and a

**Flat-Bottomed Steel Wok.** A flat-bottomed wok is particularly well-suited to an electric or heat sensor burner because the heating element comes in direct contact with the pan. The lid is necessary for steaming with a rack, or for braising.

non-metallic scrubber. The wok should be bone-dry to prevent rust, so place it on a hot burner for about 15 seconds before putting it away. Your wok will blacken with use. Besides the classic wok with ear-like handles (which has suited the Chinese for 3000 years), you can now buy a wok with one long wooden handle. You can tip and turn it with complete control as you cook, without using a potholder.

Since braziers or stoves with round openings are rare in America, you'll need a ring stand for a traditional wok. The ring fits around a gas burner, and it is perforated to allow air to enter and feed the flames. Woks work best when their bottoms are in direct contact with the heat, which presents a big problem with electric stoves. Happily, there are now a number of woks on the market with slightly flattened bottoms that sit firmly on an electric element. They come in 12- to 14-inch-diameter sizes, excellent for both stir-frying and steaming.

**Steamers:** Your wok will double as an excellent vessel for holding a steaming rack or steaming baskets. Steamed foods are among the glories of Oriental cuisines; think of a moist and delicate sea bass with scallions,

**Bamboo Steamer**. Used over boiling water in a wok, a typical multi-tiered bamboo steamer consists of two baskets and a top, in sizes ranging from 6″ to 12″ in diameter.

spicy little pearl balls stuffed with pork and bristling with grains of rice, or the delectable dumplings called *dim sum.*

To steam, the boiling water in a wok should come about an inch below the rack or first basket (use no more than two baskets to get the full effect of intense heat). Place the rack or baskets in the wok—they should be 2 inches smaller in diameter than the wok—and cover with a lid. (The high, domed lid sold with many woks is ideal if you are using a rack. Baskets usually come with their own lids.) If you put the food on a plate, necessary in a number of recipes where sauce is used, be sure that the plate is at least an inch smaller than the basket so that the clouds of steam can rise easily to envelope—and cook—the food. Steaming racks are made in metal or bamboo, but for charm nothing beats a porous lattice-work bamboo basket. There's no need for a presentation dish; the steaming basket goes directly from the stove to the table. The wood will darken with age and use, but with care—no hot water and detergents, and thorough drying plus an occasional rub with vegetable oil—bamboo will serve you well for years.

**Fire Pots:** The fire pot is a Chinese way of preparing a meal at the table.

**Aluminum Steamer.** A modern version of the bamboo steamer, this aluminum set comes with its own water container so that it can be used directly over a Western stove burner.

**Bamboo Steamer Rack.** An alternative to the steamer basket is a steamer rack. The rack — available in several sizes — is set in a wok above boiling water, a plate containing the food is set on the rack, and a cover (several inches wider than the rack) is placed over it to trap the steam.

**Brass Fire Pot**. Most fire pots are about 13″ high and hold 3 quarts of broth heated by charcoal in the base of the pot. The chimney allows heat to escape. All of the elements come apart for easy cleaning.

**Stainless-Steel Chrysanthemum Pot**. Heated by a kerosene burner in its base, this handsome pot is used at the table for heating broth in which a variety of meats and seafood are dipped and cooked.

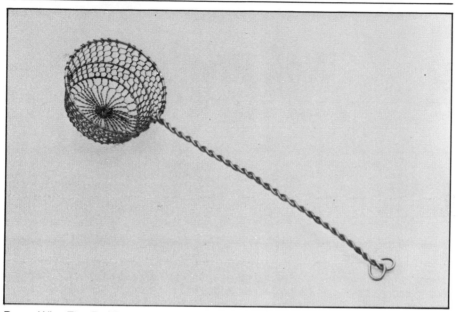

**Brass Wire Fire Pot Basket**. The tidiest way to cook food in a fire pot is with a small basket like this 9"-long one. If the handle of the basket becomes too hot to hold, the food is probably overcooked.

Perhaps our nearest equivalent is beef fondue—but fire pot food is cooked in steaming broth or water, not oil. The fire pot is said to have its origins in Mongolia, where nomads on the march dipped chunks of meat into cauldrons of boiling water. The Mongols were Mohammedans, and pork, so beloved by the Chinese, was forbidden to them. Instead, they used lamb from their extensive flocks. When the fire pot was introduced to Southern China, it became a much more elaborate dish, with guests dipping meat (everything *but* lamb), fish and vegetables into simmering broth. As each guest cooks food on a do-it-yourself basis, the broth becomes gloriously enriched. At the end of the meal, it is ladled into bowls with a little dipping sauce; and that soup is a culinary climax! There are several types of fire pot, but the Mongolian pot with the tall chimney shown on the cover is the most attractive, and can be used for all fire pot recipes, even the Japanese *shabu shabu*. To start the pot, fill the basin with broth, then add burning charcoal, with tongs, to the chimney. Start the coals outside, be sure you have an asbestos mat underneath the fire pot to protect your table, and always add the broth *before* the coals are placed in it; without the broth to absorb the heat, the solder might melt. A fire pot makes a festive family or small dinner party dish, uniting people in an elemental love of fire, fine food and companionship.

# Wok Recipes

## STIR-FRIED ASPARAGUS

Carol Cutler

6 servings

With the current popularity of authentic Chinese food in this country, many early prejudices and ideas about this sophisticated cuisine are quickly falling away. There is much we can learn about the serving of delicate flavor combinations. For instance, traditional Chinese banquets are presented one course at a time so that the individuality of each dish can be appreciated before blurring the palate with another flavor. For the busy host or hostess who prepares and serves the meal without help, this may prove impractical. But on occasion, there are certain dishes that should be spotlighted all by themselves. Stir-fried asparagus is one of them. These crunchy, bright green morsels can kick off a meal with a crisp note, or brighten the taste buds after the meat dish. On the other hand, they would compliment a cheese soufflé beautifully.

4 TABLESPOONS VEGETABLE OIL
2 TABLESPOONS SESAME SEED
 OIL (AVAILABLE IN HEALTH FOOD
 AND ORIENTAL GROCERY
 STORES)
3 SLICES FRESH GINGER
10 PEPPERCORNS
2 UNPEELED CLOVES GARLIC ,
 MASHED
1½ POUNDS FRESH ASPARAGUS
1½ TABLESPOONS SOY SAUCE
2 TABLESPOONS SHERRY
1 TEASPOON SUGAR
½ TEASPOON SALT

1. In a wok, pour in the vegetable and sesame seed oils. Add the ginger, pepper-corns, and garlic and put the pan on low heat. Cover and heat slowly to brown the garlic and ginger. This can be done well in advance.

2. Snap off and discard the tough bottom sections of the asparagus. Rinse the stalks under cold water. With a sharp knife, cut the stalks and points into long, thin diagonal slices; the longer the better.

3. In a small cup, stir together the soy sauce, sherry, sugar and salt. Make sure that the sugar has dissolved.

4. With a skimmer, remove the flavorings from the oil and heat the oil to very hot. Spill in the asparagus and turn quickly with the skimmer and a large spoon to coat all the slices with the oil. Cover the wok for 30 seconds.

5. Pour in the seasoned soy sauce and mix again thoroughly to distribute the sauce. Cover again for 30 seconds or so. Test with a small, sharp knife by piercing the center of an asparagus slice. They should remain crunchy. Spoon into a deep serving dish and serve at once.

*Note:* For calorie-conscious cooks, drain off the oil by holding the lid in place, before adding the soy sauce.

## STIR-FRIED BEAN SPROUTS

Carol Cutler

**6 servings**

When it comes to saving time, it's pretty hard to beat stir-fried bean sprouts as a vegetable dish. No slicing or peeling to do, just a quick rinse under the kitchen tap. And cooking time? One or two minutes is all it takes to turn out a fine, clean-tasting vegetable. Bean sprouts do have a characteristic flavor of their own, but rarely are we given the opportunity to taste them alone since they usually provide an inexpensive filler for meat and chicken dishes.

Until they are cooked, the sprouts are rather bulky. You may need two woks or deep skillets, or you can fry the sprouts in two batches.

2 POUNDS SOY OR MUNG BEAN
   SPROUTS
3 TABLESPOONS VEGETABLE OIL
2 TABLESPOONS SESAME SEED OIL
   (AVAILABLE IN HEALTH FOOD
   AND ORIENTAL GROCERY
   STORES)
10 PEPPERCORNS (APPROXIMATELY)
SALT
JUICE OF 1 LEMON

1. Place the sprouts in a colander or sieve and rinse them under running water. Put them aside to drain.

2. Pour the oils into the wok or skillet and add the peppercorns. Heat slowly until the oil is almost smoking hot, then remove the peppercorns with a skimmer.

3. Turn up the heat. Tip in the sprouts and begin turning them over with two large spoons to distribute the oil. Sprinkle them with salt and squeeze in the lemon juice.

4. Cover and cook for a minute or so, or just until the sprouts begin to wilt, but are still crisp. Spoon the stir-fried sprouts into a deep dish and serve at once.

# FRESH MUNG BEAN SPROUTS
## WITH MUSHROOMS

**Grace Zia Chu**

4 servings

1 POUND MUNG BEAN SPROUTS
¼ POUND FRESH MUSHROOMS
2 TABLESPOONS VEGETABLE OIL
1 TEASPOON SALT
½ TEASPOON SUGAR

1. Float the bean sprouts in a basin of cold water; remove the yellow bud on the end of the sprouts. Rinse and drain the sprouts.

2. Wash and slice the mushrooms.

3. Heat the vegetable oil in a wok. Add the mushrooms and stir-fry them for 1 minute. Add ½ teaspoon of salt and mix a few more times.

4. Add the bean sprouts to the mushrooms and stir-fry them for another minute. Add the remaining salt and the sugar. Toss again to be sure the seasoning is evenly distributed. Serve at once.


# STIR-FRIED GREEN BEANS, MUSHROOMS
## AND ONIONS

**Jeanne Lesem**

6 servings

¼ POUND FRESH MUSHROOMS
1 MEDIUM-SIZED ONION, ABOUT 2½
    INCHES IN DIAMETER
1 POUND FRESH GREEN BEANS
2 TO 3 TABLESPOONS OLIVE OIL
½ CUP WATER
1 TABLESPOON BUTTER (OPTIONAL)
SALT
FRESHLY GROUND PEPPER

1. Wipe the mushrooms clean with a damp paper towel. Slice them a scant ¼-inch thick and set them aside.

2. Peel the onion and remove both ends. Slice it lengthwise a scant ¼-inch thick. Break the slices up into strips and set them aside on a separate plate or on waxed paper.

3. Snap the ends from the green beans and break or cut them into 1½- to 2-inch lengths and set them aside on a third plate or on waxed paper.

4. Place the wok over high heat, dribbling 1 tablespoon of oil around the rim. When the oil is hot, add the mushrooms all at once. Stir constantly for about

1 minute, then remove them with a slotted spoon to a plate large enough to hold them in a single layer for quick cooling.

5. Add the onions to the wok and another tablespoon of oil, if necessary, and stir constantly while cooking for 1 minute. Using the slotted spoon, spread the onions on top of the mushrooms.

6. Add the remaining oil to the pan, add the green beans all at once, and continue to cook and stir-fry constantly over high heat until the beans are glossy and start to turn bright green.

7. Add the water and turn the heat to low immediately. (If you are using an electric range, slide the wok onto an adjoining burner heated to low; otherwise the beans will burn before they are cooked.)

8. Cover and cook for 5 to 15 minutes, depending on the age and size of the beans. Stir occasionally. When the beans are almost tender, remove the cover and add the mushrooms and onions. Turn the heat to high and stir constantly for 1 minute to reheat the mushrooms and onions, and to evaporate the liquid remaining in the pan.

9. Add the butter if you are using it and stir to blend. Transfer the vegetables to a serving dish and serve at once. Allow each guest to salt and pepper the mixture to taste.

*Note:* If you omit the butter from this recipe, leftovers can be made into a quick salad by dribbling them with vinegar or lemon juice and a speck of grated fresh garlic.

## STIR-FRIED ZUCCHINI

Emanuel and Madeline Greenberg

2 to 4 servings

1 POUND MEDIUM-SIZED ZUCCHINI
  (ABOUT 4 TO THE POUND)
1 TO 2 TABLESPOONS OLIVE OIL
1 LARGE CLOVE GARLIC,
  SLIVERED
SALT
FRESHLY GROUND PEPPER
1 TABLESPOON FINELY CHOPPED
  FRESH BASIL OR PARSLEY

1. Trim off the ends of the zucchini. Scrub the zucchini and cut it into lengthwise quarters, then into crosswise pieces about 2 inches long.

2. Heat the oil in the wok over medium-high heat. Add the zucchini and stir-fry about 1 minute. Add the garlic slivers, the salt and pepper to taste, and continue stirring until the zucchini is lightly browned and just tender, 3 to 5 minutes. Sprinkle with basil or parsley and stir through.

# SZECHUAN EGGPLANT

**Carole Lalli**

4 servings

1 MEDIUM-SIZED EGGPLANT, ABOUT 1½ POUNDS
2 TEASPOONS SALT
2 TEASPOONS SOY OR OTHER VEGETABLE OIL
¼ POUND MINCED OR GROUND PORK
3 OR 4 LARGE CLOVES GARLIC, CRUSHED WITH THE SIDE OF A CLEAVER OR LARGE KNIFE
2 OR 3 SCALLIONS, CUT IN ½-INCH LENGTHS
1 TEASPOON SESAME OIL
¼ TO ½ TEASPOON CRUSHED RED PEPPER
1 TABLESPOON DARK SOY SAUCE

1. Peel and cut the eggplant into strips about 1-inch wide and 2 or 3 inches long. Sprinkle it lightly with salt and drain on paper towels for 30 minutes or more and pat it dry.

2. Heat the vegetable oil in the wok and add the pork, stirring and cooking just until it loses its color.

3. Add the garlic and scallions, and stir-fry for about 30 seconds.

4. Add the eggplant, the sesame oil and the hot red pepper; stir-fry for another 30 seconds, then turn down the heat, cover the wok and cook for about 15 to 20 minutes, stirring occasionally. The eggplant should be very tender, almost the consistency of a purée.

5. Add the soy sauce just before serving.

# WINTER VEGETABLES IN THE WOK

**Michael Batterberry**

4 to 6 servings

This is very good with fish or chicken in cream.

2 MEDIUM-SIZED CARROTS, SCRAPED
3 TABLESPOONS OLIVE OIL
½ POUND FIRM WHITE MUSHROOMS, CUT INTO THICK MATCHSTICKS
1 TABLESPOON COGNAC
½ CLOVE GARLIC, MINCED
3 DROPS LEMON JUICE
½ TEASPOON COARSE SALT
2 TABLESPOONS BUTTER (PREFERABLY UNSALTED)
½ POUND WHITE TURNIPS, CUT INTO THICK MATCHSTICKS
¼ CUP CHICKEN STOCK
CELERY CUT INTO THICK MATCHSTICKS; ENOUGH TO MAKE 2 CUPS
½ TEASPOON THYME
⅛ TEASPOON FRESHLY GRATED NUTMEG
1 TABLESPOON CHOPPED PARSLEY
1 TABLESPOON CHOPPED DILL
FRESHLY GROUND WHITE PEPPER

1. Holding the tip of a carrot with your left hand, scrape off as many long ribbons as possible—you'll be left with a nubbin and the hard, pale, woody core. Discard these leftovers.

2. Heat 1 tablespoon of oil over high heat in a wok. When the oil is smoking, throw in the mushroom slices and stir-fry them over medium heat for 2 to 3 minutes. After the first 2 minutes, season them with cognac, garlic, lemon juice, and ½ teaspoon of salt. Remove and set them aside.

3. Wipe the wok and, over medium heat, melt 2 tablespoons of butter in the remaining oil. Turn the heat higher and add the turnips. Stir-fry them for 4 minutes, add the chicken stock, cover the wok and cook 1½ minutes longer.

4. Remove the cover, add the celery and thyme and cook 2 minutes more.

5. Add the carrot ribbons and nutmeg and cook 15 to 30 seconds. Sprinkle with herbs and white pepper to taste. Toss and serve.

# VEGETABLE MEDLEY

Maurice Moore-Betty

3 to 4 servings

2 CARROTS
1 SMALL CELERY ROOT
2 SMALL TURNIPS
½ POUND VERY YOUNG GREEN
    BEANS
3 SMALL ZUCCHINI
BUTTER AND OIL IN EQUAL
    QUANTITIES
1 TEASPOON VEGETABLE SEASON-
    ING SALT
1 HANDFUL WATERCRESS LEAVES

1. Peel and cut the carrots, celery root and turnips into matchsticks. Wash, top and tail the green beans and slit them lengthwise. Wash the zucchini and cut it into matchsticks.

2. Heat 1 tablespoon of oil and 1 of butter in the wok.

3. Add the carrots, celery root, turnips and beans and quickly stir-fry them. Add more oil and butter as needed. The heat should be high and the stir-frying constant.

4. Test now and again; as soon as the vegetables soften slightly, throw in the zucchini and the seasoning salt. Stir-fry for a minute or so longer.

5. Just before serving, stir in the watercress leaves. Serve immediately.

# STIR-FRIED GARDEN VEGETABLES

Ruth Ellen Church

4 servings

½ POUND MUSHROOMS, SLICED
2 SMALL YOUNG CARROTS,
  SCRAPED, SLICED THIN
  CROSSWISE
6 ZUCCHINI ABOUT 6-INCHES
  LONG, SLICED DIAGONALLY
  ¼-INCH THICK
1 LEEK, WELL WASHED, SLICED
  THIN, WITH TENDER PART OF
  TOP OR 4 SLICED SCALLIONS
  WITH TOPS

6 CHERRY TOMATOES, CUT IN
  HALF
3 TABLESPOONS PEANUT OR
  SAFFLOWER OIL FOR WOK
¼ CUP CHICKEN BROTH
1 TABLESPOON LEMON JUICE
SALT TO TASTE
WHITE PEPPER TO TASTE

1. Rub the mushrooms clean with a crumpled piece of paper toweling before slicing. Prepare the vegetables first and keep them separate.

2. With the ingredients at hand, heat the wok and add the oil. When hot, stir-fry the carrots for 1 minute, then add the zucchini and leek. Stir-fry 2 minutes longer. Add the mushrooms and stir briefly.

3. Add the broth and cover the wok for 2 or 3 minutes.

4. Add the tomatoes, heat through and season with lemon juice, salt and pepper.


# STIR-FRIED CHINESE VEGETABLES

Emanuel and Madeline Greenberg

4 to 6 servings

1 POUND BEAN SPROUTS
VEGETABLE OIL
¼ POUND MUSHROOMS, CUT IN
  LARGE PIECES
¼ POUND GREEN BEANS, CUT IN
  1-INCH PIECES
1 LARGE ONION, HALVED AND
  THINLY SLICED
1 CLOVE GARLIC, CRUSHED
1 TEASPOON GRATED FRESH
  GINGER

¼ POUND SNOW PEAS, TRIMMED
  (OPTIONAL)
6 TO 8 CANNED WATER
  CHESTNUTS, SLICED
1 TABLESPOON SOY SAUCE
1 TEASPOON SESAME OIL (AVAIL-
  ABLE IN HEALTH FOOD AND
  ORIENTAL GROCERY STORES)
SALT TO TASTE
· PEPPER TO TASTE

1. Place the bean sprouts in a colander and pour boiling water over them. Immediately rinse them with cold water.

2. Heat about 1 tablespoon of oil in the wok over medium-high heat. Add the mushrooms and stir-fry until they brown lightly and most of their liquid has evaporated. Remove them from the wok.

3. Pour about 1 or 2 tablespoons of vegetable oil in the wok. Add the green

beans and stir-fry about 1 minute. Add the bean sprouts, onion, garlic and ginger. Stir-fry about 2 minutes. Add the mushrooms, snow peas and water chestnuts. Heat through.

4. Stir in the soy sauce, sesame oil, salt and pepper.

---

# SHRIMP "STRAWBERRIES"

**Michael Tong**

12 "strawberries"

½ POUND FRESH SHRIMP, SHELLED, DEVEINED AND WASHED
2 WATER CHESTNUTS, SHELLED IF FRESH
1 EGG WHITE
1¼ TEASPOONS SALT
¼ TEASPOON MONOSODIUM GLUTAMATE (MSG) (OPTIONAL)

1 TABLESPOON DRY SHERRY
1 TABLESPOON CORNSTARCH
1 TEASPOON SESAME OIL
1 CUP WHITE SESAME SEEDS
DROPS OF RED FOOD COLORING
½ FRESH GREEN BELL PEPPER
5 CUPS SALAD OIL

1. Chop the shrimp into very fine pieces. Continue chopping until the shrimp is almost a paste, then put it in a bowl.

2. Chop the water chestnuts very fine and add them to the shrimp.

3. Add the egg white, salt, monosodium glutamate (if using), sherry, cornstarch and sesame oil to the shrimp and blend well. Put the mixture in the refrigerator for at least 30 minutes.

4. Spread the sesame seeds on a long, flat ovenproof plate. Add the red food coloring to the seeds. Blend until all the seeds are evenly colored. Dry the seeds by putting them in the oven at 200 F. for 5 minutes.

5. Slice the green pepper into ¼-inch strips, about 1-inch long, to be used as stems.

6. Remove the shrimp mixture from the refrigerator. Take about 1 tablespoon of the mixture in the palm of your hand. Squeeze your thumb and forefinger, pushing the mixture up through the opening created by your fingers. Scoop off the mixture with your other hand and place it on the sesame seeds. Repeat this procedure until all the shrimp mixture has been used, allowing an inch between each "strawberry."

7. Roll each "strawberry" in the sesame seeds, completely covering each one.

8. Add the green pepper slice (stem) to the top of the shrimp strawberries. Put them in the refrigerator for 1 hour to firm them.

9. In a wok, heat the oil to 400 F. for 5 minutes. Place the shrimp "strawberries" in the oil. Lower the heat to 300 F. Fry them for 5 minutes. Raise the heat to 400 F. Fry them for 3 more minutes. Remove them and drain. Serve hot.

---

# STIR-FRIED SHRIMP AND OKRA

Raymond Sokolov

4 servings

½ POUND OKRA, FRESH OR
 FROZEN
4 TABLESPOONS OIL
1 TABLESPOON MINCED FRESH
 GINGER ROOT
2 TABLESPOONS SLICED
 SCALLIONS
1 CLOVE GARLIC, CHOPPED
1 POUND SHRIMP, SHELLED AND
 DEVEINED

1. Cut the stems off the okra.

2. Heat the oil in a wok over high heat until it begins to smoke. Immediately add the okra and ginger and stir-fry for 1 minute.

3. Add all other ingredients and stir-fry until the shrimp have just cooked through.

# CARP ROE CROQUETTES IN THE GREEK MANNER (TARAMOKEFTEDES)

Vilma Liacouras Chantiles

30 to 35 croquettes

Bright orange carp roe (*tarama*) is available in Greek or Japanese specialty stores. The roe and potatoes produce a delectable, soft interior with a crisp exterior. Laced with lemon and herbs, the fish flavor is balanced.

If you wish to reduce the saltiness of the roe, place it in a strainer that has been lined with dampened cheesecloth. Slowly run cold water over the roe for 1 minute. Allow it to drain thoroughly.

¾ CUP CARP ROE (*TARAMA*)
2 MEDIUM-SIZED POTATOES,
 BOILED IN JACKETS UNTIL
 TENDER (ABOUT 15 MINUTES)
BREAD CRUMBS OR FINE BURGHUL
 WHEAT
2 TO 3 TABLESPOONS MINCED
 FRESH PARSLEY
2 TO 3 TABLESPOONS MINCED
 FRESH DILL, OR 1½ TABLE-
 SPOONS DRIED MINT, CRUMBLED

JUICE OF ½ TO 1 LEMON,
 STRAINED
BLACK PEPPER
1 EGG, LIGHTLY BEATEN
2 CUPS PLUS 1 TEASPOON LIGHT
 VEGETABLE OIL
2 TO 3 SCALLIONS INCLUDING
 SOME GREEN, MINCED
ALL-PURPOSE FLOUR (OPTIONAL)

1. Place the roe in a mixing bowl. Peel the potatoes while hot and add them to the roe, mashing with a fork. The mixture will be too thin to mound. Add

20

enough bread crumbs or pounded fine burghul wheat to thicken it. Beating with a wooden spoon, add the parsley, dill, lemon juice, a few grindings of pepper, and half of the egg. (Save the other half for another use.)

2. In a 14-inch wok, heat 1 teaspoon of the oil and sauté the scallions until the green part brightens. Stir them into the roe mixture, knead for 1 minute and taste for flavor. The mixture should have a nice, herby tang. Cover and refrigerate it for a few hours, if possible.

3. When you are ready to fry, shape the croquettes into small balls, smaller than walnuts, rolling them in flour for a crustier product.

4. In the wok, heat the 2 cups of oil to 365 F. Slip six balls into the oil and fry them for 30 seconds, undisturbed. Using a spatula, turn the balls and keep turning them to fry evenly. Using a Chinese strainer or slotted spoon, remove them to a warm platter and keep warm. Add six more balls and continue frying. Avoid overheating the oil. When all the croquettes have been fried, remove the wok from the heat.

5. Serve the *taramokeftedes* hot as an appetizer or entrée.

6. Cool the oil. Strain it and use it again for frying fish.

---

# STIR-FRIED SHRIMP IN THE SHELL

Joanne Will

4 appetizer servings

1 POUND SHRIMP IN SHELLS
  (ABOUT 16)
2 TABLESPOONS LIGHT SOY SAUCE
2 TABLESPOONS DRY SHERRY
2 TEASPOONS MINCED GARLIC
2 TEASPOONS MINCED FRESH
  GINGER
1 TEASPOON SUGAR
2 TABLESPOONS OIL
2 SCALLIONS INCLUDING GREEN
  PART, MINCED

1. Rinse the shrimp under cold running water. Remove the legs, leaving the shells intact. With a sharp knife or scissors, carefully slit the shell along the back of each shrimp. Remove the vein with a knife tip or toothpick. Rinse the shrimp and pat them dry with paper towels.

2. Place the shrimp in a bowl with the soy sauce, sherry, garlic, ginger, and sugar. Let them stand 10 to 15 minutes to develop flavors, stirring occasionally.

3. Heat a wok or large heavy skillet. Add the oil and heat it. Add the shrimp in one layer. Cook, stirring and turning, until the shrimp are cooked and the shells are browned (about 5 minutes).

4. Sprinkle the shrimp with the scallions. Serve hot or cold as an appetizer.

# SEA SCALLOPS WITH CUCUMBERS AND TARRAGON

Elizabeth Colchie

3 servings

3 TABLESPOONS PEANUT OIL
1¼ POUNDS SEA SCALLOPS,
  SLICED HORIZONTALLY INTO
  ¼-INCH-THICK ROUNDS
3 TABLESPOONS DRY VERMOUTH
1 TEASPOON SALT
3 SLICED SCALLIONS
1½ TEASPOONS DRIED TARRAGON

2 CUCUMBERS, PEELED, SLICED
  LENGTHWISE, CORED AND CUT
  CROSSWISE INTO CRESCENTS
  ¼-INCH THICK
½ TEASPOON SUGAR
1½ TEASPOONS CORNSTARCH
2 TABLESPOONS WATER

1. Have all the ingredients ready.

2. Heat the wok over high heat. Pour in 2 tablespoons of oil around the rim. Stir-fry the scallops for 1 minute, adding the vermouth and salt and transfer the scallops to a dish.

3. Add the remaining oil and heat it. Add the scallions, tarragon, and cucumbers and stir-fry them for 2 to 3 minutes.

4. Stir together the sugar, cornstarch and water; add the mixture to the wok with the scallops and their liquid. Stir for 30 seconds or so and season.


# STIR-FRIED SHRIMP WITH PEA PODS IN OYSTER SAUCE

Paul Rubinstein

4 servings

¾ POUND FRESH SHRIMP
  (MEDIUM-SIZED)
2 TEASPOONS CORNSTARCH
1 TABLESPOON MADEIRA WINE
¼ TEASPOON SALT
1 POUND FRESH OR FROZEN
  SNOW PEA PODS
3 TABLESPOONS PEANUT OIL
¾ CUP OYSTER SAUCE (AVAIL-
  ABLE IN ORIENTAL GROCERIES)
3 SCALLIONS, MINCED

1. Peel and devein the shrimp, then wash them in cold water and pat them dry with paper towels.

2. Combine the cornstarch, Madeira and salt in a mixing bowl, add the shrimp, and toss to coat them with the liquid.

3. Cut off the tips and remove the strings from the pea pods.

4. Heat 1½ tablespoons of the peanut oil in a wok over medium heat. Add the shrimp and stir-fry for 2 minutes until they are pink. Remove the shrimp from the wok and set them aside.

5. Add the remaining peanut oil to the wok and stir-fry the pea pods over medium heat for about 4 minutes, stirring frequently.

6. Pour off most of the oil, return the shrimp to the wok, add the oyster sauce and minced scallions and mix well. Cover and cook about 3 minutes, until it is simmering.

7. Serve immediately with rice.


# FRIED RICE WITH SHRIMP AND HAM

Paula J. Buchholz

**6 servings**

4⅓ TABLESPOONS SALAD OIL
1 EGG, BEATEN
4 SCALLIONS, THINLY SLICED,
 INCLUDING GREEN PART
¼ POUND COOKED TINY SHRIMP
¼ POUND COOKED HAM, DICED
1 CUP FRESH BEAN SPROUTS
3 CUPS COLD COOKED RICE
½ CUP FRESH OR FROZEN AND
 THAWED PEAS
2 TABLESPOONS OYSTER SAUCE
2 TABLESPOONS SOY SAUCE
SALT TO TASTE
PEPPER TO TASTE

1. Heat the wok. Dribble 1 teaspoon of oil into the wok.

2. Stir-fry the beaten egg, just until it is set, about 20 seconds. Remove the egg and set it aside.

3. Add 2 tablespoons of oil to the wok and reheat it. Stir-fry the scallions, shrimp, ham and bean sprouts for a minute or two. Remove and set them aside.

4. Add 2 more tablespoons of oil to the wok and heat. Stir-fry the rice, breaking up any lumps.

5. Add all of the other ingredients, including the egg; cook and stir until the fried rice is well mixed and heated through.

# CHICKEN SUPREMES WITH VINEGAR AND HERBS

Julie Dannenbaum

4 servings

2 WHOLE CHICKEN BREASTS,
  SKINNED AND BONED
¼ CUP FLOUR
SALT
FRESHLY GROUND BLACK PEPPER
2 TABLESPOONS OIL
1 TEASPOON CRUSHED ROSEMARY
3 TABLESPOONS WINE VINEGAR
1 TABLESPOON FINELY CHOPPED
  PARSLEY

1. Cut the chicken into thin strips and toss them in the flour, seasoned with salt and pepper.

2. Heat the wok and add the oil.

3. When the oil is hot, add the chicken strips and toss them for 3 to 5 minutes.

4. Add the rosemary and vinegar and cook 2 to 3 minutes longer.

5. Sprinkle with the parsley and serve.


# STIR-FRIED CHICKEN AND GREEN PEPPERS

Gloria Bley Miller

2 servings

1 LARGE OR 2 SMALL CHICKEN
  BREASTS
1 TABLESPOON PLUS 2 TEASPOONS
  CORNSTARCH
2½ TABLESPOONS MEDIUM-DRY
  SHERRY
1½ TABLESPOONS SOY SAUCE
2 GREEN PEPPERS
1 SCALLION
1 CLOVE GARLIC
1 TEASPOON SALT
¼ CUP PLUS 2 TABLESPOONS
  CHICKEN STOCK
2 TO 3 TABLESPOONS PEANUT OIL

1. Skin and bone the chicken breasts, then cut them in 1-inch cubes.

2. In a bowl, combine the 1 tablespoon of the cornstarch, 1½ tablespoons of sherry and ½ tablespoon of soy sauce. Add the chicken and toss to coat it. Let it stand for 30 minutes, turning occasionally.

3. Meanwhile, cut the green peppers in half. Discard the seeds, then cut them in 1-inch squares. Cut the scallion in 1-inch lengths. Mince the garlic.

4. Bring water to a boil in a pan. Add ½ teaspoon of salt, then the diced peppers. Parboil for 2 minutes. Drain at once in a colander or sieve and cool under cold running water. Drain them again.

5. In one cup, combine ¼ cup of the stock and the remaining sherry and soy sauce. In another cup, blend the remaining cornstarch and stock.

6. Heat a wok. Add the oil and heat it. Add the remaining salt, then the minced garlic. When the garlic turns golden, add the chicken and stir-fry it until it turns white.

7. Add the diced peppers, stir-frying to heat them through. Add the stock-sherry-soy sauce mixture, stir-frying to blend it in. Cover the wok and let everything cook for 2 minutes.

8. Restir the cornstarch mixture, then add it to the pan. Cook, stirring, until the sauce thickens. Serve at once.

# CHICKEN WITH SZECHUAN PICKLE

Florence Fabricant

2 to 4 servings

3 TABLESPOONS COOKING OIL
1 SLICE FRESH GINGER, MINCED
1 SCALLION, CHOPPED
1 CLOVE GARLIC, MINCED
6 OUNCES SKINLESS AND BONE-
　LESS CHICKEN BREAST, MINCED
1½ TABLESPOONS MINCED CELERY
1 WATER CHESTNUT, MINCED
2 FRESH MEDIUM-SIZED MUSH-
　ROOMS, MINCED
½ RED BELL PEPPER, MINCED
¼ CUP MINCED BAMBOO SHOOTS*
4 SNOW PEA PODS, MINCED

¼ CUP CANNED SZECHUAN
　PICKLED VEGETABLE,* MINCED
1 TEASPOON SOY SAUCE
SALT
FRESHLY GROUND PEPPER
½ TEASPOON SUGAR
1 TEASPOON SHERRY
1 TEASPOON CORNSTARCH
　DISSOLVED IN 1 TABLESPOON
　COLD WATER
½ TEASPOON HOT CHILI OIL*
1 TABLESPOON PINE NUTS

1. Heat the wok for 30 seconds, add the oil and then add the ginger, scallion, garlic and the chicken. Stir-fry for 2 to 3 minutes. Remove the ingredients from the wok with a skimmer and set them aside.

2. Add the celery, water chestnut, mushrooms, red pepper, bamboo shoots, snow peas, Szechuan pickle, soy sauce, salt and pepper to taste, sugar and sherry to the wok and stir-fry for 1 minute. Add the cornstarch mixture, stir , then return the chicken, ginger, scallion and garlic to the wok. Add the hot chili oil. Stir. Transfer the chicken to a serving platter, sprinkle it with pine nuts and serve.

* These ingredients are available in Oriental grocery stores.

# SPICY CHICKEN WITH TANGERINE FLAVOR

## Carole Lalli

4 servings

¼ CUP RICE WINE OR DRY WHITE
WINE
2 TABLESPOONS SOY SAUCE
1 TABLESPOON CHINESE OR
OTHER VINEGAR
2 WHOLE CHICKEN BREASTS,
SKINNED AND BONED
1 TABLESPOON SOY OR OTHER
VEGETABLE OIL

1 TABLESPOON DARK SESAME OIL*
RIND (ORANGE PART ONLY) OF A
TANGERINE OR A BRIGHT-
SKINNED ORANGE
4 OR 5 WHOLE, DRIED HOT RED
CHILI PEPPERS
¼ TEASPOON SZECHUAN PEPPER,*
CRUSHED (OPTIONAL)

1. Make a marinade of the wine, soy sauce and vinegar. Cut the chicken into strips about ½-inch by 2 inches, and add to the marinade for 30 minutes or more.

2. Heat the soy and sesame oils in the wok; cook the rind and the chili peppers for a few minutes. The rind should be slightly scorched.

3. Drain the chicken and reserve the marinade. Stir-fry the chicken in the oil for about a minute, then add the Szechuan pepper (if you are using it) and the reserved marinade and cook for about 1 more minute. The rind may be eaten, but the hot red peppers should be avoided.

*These ingredients are available in Oriental grocery stores.

# CHICKEN WITH SNOW PEA PODS

## Grace Zia Chu

4 servings

1 WHOLE CHICKEN BREAST
1 TEASPOON SALT
1 TABLESPOON DRY SHERRY
1 TEASPOON CORNSTARCH
3 TABLESPOONS VEGETABLE OIL
10 OUNCES FRESH SNOW PEA
PODS, TRIMMED AND CUT INTO
1-INCH PIECES
½ CUP WATER CHESTNUT SLICES
(8 WATER CHESTNUTS)

1. Skin and bone the chicken breast. Freeze it long enough to firm it for easy slicing. Then carefully slice it into 1-by-½-by-¼-inch pieces.

2. Mix the chicken slices with ½ teaspoon salt and the sherry, then stir in the cornstarch.

3. Heat 1 tablespoon of oil in a wok. Stir-fry the snow pea pods for 20 seconds.

Add ½ teaspoon of salt. Mix them a few more times. Add the water chestnut slices and stir-fry for another 10 seconds. Set them aside.

4. Heat 2 more tablespoons of oil in the wok. When the oil is hot, add the chicken mixture. Quickly stir, separating the pieces with chopsticks. Keep stir-frying until all the chicken pieces turn opaque.

5. Return the snow peas and water chestnuts to the wok. Mix a few times and serve.

*Note:* If snow peas are not available, you may substitute 2 cups of shredded green or red sweet pepper.

# TURKEY IN THE WOK

Michael Batterberry

4 servings

3 CLOVES GARLIC, HALVED LENGTHWISE
4 TABLESPOONS PEANUT OIL
3 TABLESPOONS SESAME OIL*
4 CUPS CUBED COOKED TURKEY (THE LARGER THE CUBES THE BETTER)
1 CUP WALNUT HALVES OR LARGE PIECES
CHINESE HOT OIL*
½ POUND SNOW PEAS
8 SCALLIONS IN ¾-INCH LENGTHS
2 TEASPOONS MINCED FRESH GINGER
1 TABLESPOON SOY SAUCE, PREFERABLY KIKKOMAN
1 TABLESPOON DRY SHERRY

1. Slowly heat together the garlic, 3 tablespoons of the peanut oil and 1 tablespoon of the sesame oil until the garlic turns golden. Remove the garlic and discard it.

2. Turn the heat to high and add the turkey, tossing for 2 to 3 minutes, depending on the size of the cubes. The turkey must be hot all the way through. Remove it from the oil with a wire mesh ladle or a slotted spoon.

3. Add another tablespoon of sesame oil to the wok; over medium heat, cook the walnuts, stirring constantly to avoid scorching, until they are visibly darker. Sprinkle with drops of hot oil to taste and remove them. Be sure that no little pieces of nut remain behind.

4. Add 1 more tablespoon each of sesame and peanut oil, turn up the heat and stir-fry the snow peas and scallions for 1 minute.

5. Add the ginger and continue to cook for 30 seconds.

6. Add the soy sauce and sherry and return the turkey and walnuts to the wok. Toss 10 seconds more and ladle out into a heated serving dish. Adjust the soy sauce if necessary.

* These ingredients are available in Oriental grocery stores.

# CHICKEN AND CASHEWS

**Harvey Steiman**

4 to 6 servings

2 BONED AND SKINNED CHICKEN
BREASTS, CUT INTO STRIPS
1 TABLESPOON *HOISIN* SAUCE*
2 TABLESPOONS SOY SAUCE
2 TEASPOONS SHERRY
2 TEASPOONS CORNSTARCH
DASH OF WHITE PEPPER
½ TEASPOON SESAME OIL*

1 EGG WHITE
3 TABLESPOONS VEGETABLE OIL
1 CUP DRY-ROASTED CASHEWS
2 SCALLIONS, MINCED
1 CLOVE GARLIC, CRUSHED
½ CUP DICED BAMBOO SHOOTS*
½ CUP GINGKO NUTS* (OPTIONAL)

1. Mix the chicken with the *hoisin,* soy, sherry, cornstarch, pepper, sesame oil and egg white. Marinate it for 30 minutes.

2. Heat 1½ tablespoons of oil in a wok for 30 seconds over high heat. Add the cashews and stir-fry them for 30 seconds. Set them aside.

3. Heat the remaining oil in the wok for 30 seconds. Add the scallions and garlic stir-fry them for 10 seconds. Add chicken mixture; stir-fry until the chicken browns slightly and turns opaque. Add the cashews, bamboo shoots and the gingkos. Heat through and serve.

   * These ingredients are available in Oriental grocery stores.

# BEEF WITH BROCCOLI

**Joanne Will**

4 servings

1 POUND BEEF FLANK STEAK
1 TEASPOON MINCED GARLIC
1 TEASPOON MINCED FRESH
GINGER
¼ CUP DRY SHERRY PLUS 1
TEASPOON
2 TABLESPOONS LIGHT SOY SAUCE
PLUS 1 TEASPOON

2 CUPS PARED AND TRIMMED
BROCCOLI STEMS
3 SCALLIONS, CHOPPED
1 TEASPOON SUGAR
2 TEASPOONS CORNSTARCH
3 TABLESPOONS OIL
⅔ CUP BEEF BROTH

1. Put the beef in the freezer and chill it until it is firm enough to cut into thin slices. (This will take about an hour.) Cut the steak in half, lengthwise; then cut each half across the grain (with your cleaver or knife angled or slanted) into very thin slices. Put the slices in a bowl to marinate with the garlic, ginger, ¼ cup of the sherry and 2 tablespoons of the soy sauce.

2. Cut off the broccoli florets and reserve them for another use. Trim the base of each stem and peel off the tough skin. Cut the stems lengthwise into halves or quarters (depending on thickness) and then cut them diagonally into 2-inch pieces.

3. Bring a pot of water to the boil and put in the broccoli pieces. As soon as the water returns to the boil, drain the broccoli and reserve it.

4. Cut the scallions into 1-inch pieces.

5. In a small cup, combine the sugar, the remaining teaspoon of soy sauce, the sherry and cornstarch and mix well.

6. Heat the wok and pour in 1½ tablespoons of the oil. When it is hot, add the beef and stir-fry for 1 minute. Remove the meat and pour off the liquid.

7 Return the wok to the heat and pour in the remaining oil. Tip in the broccoli and stir-fry it for 30 seconds. Pour in the broth and bring it just to the boil.

8. Immediately add the beef and the cornstarch mixture to the broccoli and cook, stirring, until it is slightly thickened. Add the scallions and serve at once.

# STEAK WITH PEPPERS AND MUSHROOMS (MANZO PEPERONATA)

Nicola Zanghi

**4 servings**

You can use sirloin shell steak, porterhouse or filet mignon for this recipe. Make sure the meat is very well trimmed.

½ CUP OLIVE OIL
1 CUP THINLY SLICED ONIONS
1 CUP THIN GREEN PEPPER STRIPS
1 CUP SLICED FRESH MUSHROOMS
2 POUNDS SIRLOIN STEAK CUT
   INTO ½-INCH STRIPS
1½ CUPS DICED PLUM TOMATOES,
   SEEDED AND JUICED
½ TEASPOON OREGANO
½ TEASPOON BASIL
SALT
FRESHLY GROUND PEPPER

1. Heat the wok and pour in ¼ cup of oil. When it is hot, add the onions and stir-fry them until they are limp and translucent. Add the peppers and continue to stir-fry until they are limp. Tip in the mushrooms and toss and stir until they are lightly browned. With a slotted spoon, remove the vegetables to a platter and pour off the oil.

2. Pour in the remaining oil and when it is hot and a haze forms over it, stir in the meat and brown it quickly.

3. Return the vegetables to the wok and add the tomatoes and herbs. Stir for 1 minute. Season with salt and pepper to taste.

# CHINESE BARBECUED SPARE RIBS

Paula J. Buchholz

6 servings

1 3- TO 4-POUND SLAB OF PORK
  SPARERIBS
WATER
1 TABLESPOON RICE WINE
  VINEGAR
½ CUP SOY SAUCE
¼ CUP FIRMLY-PACKED BROWN
  SUGAR
2 TABLESPOONS CORNSTARCH
  DISSOLVED IN ⅔ CUP COLD
  WATER

1. Have the butcher chop the slab of ribs horizontally into 1-inch pieces. Cut between the bones to separate them into individual pieces.

2. Heat the wok.

3. Add the ribs and about ¼ cup of water to the wok. Slowly cook the ribs, turning them frequently, until they are cooked through and well browned. (You will have to cook them in several batches.) When they are done, remove them to a platter.

4. Combine the rice wine, soy sauce, brown sugar and another ½ cup of water in the wok. Heat the mixture and slowly pour in the dissolved cornstarch, cooking and stirring, until the mixture is thickened.

5. Return the ribs to the wok and heat through. Serve hot or chill and serve them cold.

# CHOPPED BEEF OMELET IN THE WOK

Grace Zia Chu

4 servings

½ TEASPOON MINCED FRESH
  GINGER
3 TEASPOONS DRY SHERRY
2 TEASPOONS DARK SOY SAUCE
2 TEASPOONS PEANUT OIL PLUS
  4 TABLESPOONS
2 TEASPOONS CORNSTARCH
1 TABLESPOON COLD WATER
½ POUND GROUND ROUND STEAK
4 EGGS
½ TEASPOON SALT

1. Combine the ginger, 2 teaspoons of the sherry, the soy sauce, 2 teaspoons

of oil, the cornstarch and cold water. Pour them over the meat and let the mixture marinate for at least 10 minutes.

2. Beat the eggs until they are well mixed. Add the salt and remaining sherry. Beat a little more and set aside.

3. Heat the wok and add 2 tablespoons of the oil. As soon as it is hot, add the marinated meat and stir-fry for about 2 minutes. Remove the meat from the wok and mix it into the eggs.

4. Wipe out the wok, add the remaining oil and heat. When the oil is hot, pour in the combined eggs and meat. Over a medium flame, let the eggs set until they are firm enough to turn over. Flip the eggs and after a few seconds, turn the omelet onto a serving plate.

---

# PORK WITH PEPPERS, BROCCOLI AND ONIONS

Jane Moulton

4 to 6 servings

1 POUND LEAN PORK
1 TEASPOON SALT
¼ TEASPOON SUGAR
2 CLOVES GARLIC, PEELED AND MINCED
4 TABLESPOONS VEGETABLE OIL
3 TABLESPOONS DRY SHERRY
3 TABLESPOONS SOY SAUCE
1 LARGE SPANISH ONION, PEELED, QUARTERED AND CUT INTO ¾-INCH PIECES
2 SWEET PEPPERS (ONE GREEN AND ONE RED, IF POSSIBLE), SEEDED AND CUT INTO ¼-INCH STRIPS

2 CUPS BROCCOLI FLORETS
1 SMALL BUNCH CHINESE CABBAGE (BOK CHOY), CUT INTO 1½-INCH PIECES
2 CUPS SLICED FRESH MUSHROOMS
½ CUP BEEF STOCK
1½ TABLESPOONS CORNSTARCH
HOT RICE

1. Cut the pork into paper thin slices about 1½ to 2 inches long. Mix into the meat the salt, sugar and garlic.

2. Heat a wok and add 2 tablespoons of oil. When it is hot, stir-fry the pork mixture just until it loses its pink color. Pour the meat and juices into a bowl and stir in the 3 tablespoons each of sherry and soy sauce.

3. Reheat the wok. Pour in the remaining oil and when it is hot, stir-fry the onion for about 1 minute. Keep the heat high and add the peppers, broccoli, cabbage and mushrooms, lifting to mix well after each addition. Add the meat and its juice and the combined beef stock and cornstarch. Lift and stir to mix it well.

4. Cover the wok and steam for about 3 minutes. Serve the pork and vegetables with hot rice.

---

# LAMB AND ARTICHOKES, CRETAN STYLE
## (KREAS KAI ANGINARES AVGOLEMONO
## ME PLIGOURI)

Vilma Liacouras Chantiles

4 to 6 servings

Cretans enjoy aniseed in their meats and vegetables, as well as in some desserts. I have adapted this popular dish and its accompaniment, *pligouri* (cracked wheat), for the wok and steamer.

1 POUND LEAN LAMB, CUT INTO
  STRIPS
STRAINED JUICE FROM 1½
  LEMONS
¾ CUP MEDIUM-FINE *BURGHUL*
  OR OTHER CRACKED WHEAT
1 TO 2 TABLESPOONS VEGETABLE
  OIL

SALT
FRESHLY GROUND PEPPER
1½ TEASPOONS ANISEED
12 SMALL FRESH ARTICHOKES,
  QUARTERED, OR 2 PACKAGES
  FROZEN ARTICHOKES, DE-
  FROSTED AND HALVED
2 EGG YOLKS

1. Marinate the lamb in 1 tablespoon of the lemon juice for 1 hour or longer. Then drain it and pat it dry.

2. Pour boiling water over the cracked wheat and soak it for 15 minutes or more.

3. Heat a wok and dribble in 1 tablespoon of the oil. When the oil is hot, add the meat and stir-fry it for 3 to 4 minutes, or until the meat changes color. Season with salt, pepper and 1 teaspoon of the aniseed. Scoop the meat from the wok onto a warm platter and keep it warm.

4. Add the artichokes to the wok, enough water to almost cover them, and the remaining aniseed.

5. Spread a dampened length of doubled cheesecloth (or a napkin) in a steamer basket and spread the drained wheat over the cloth. Set the steamer over the artichokes, cover it, and simmer for 20 minutes, or until the artichokes are tender.

6. Remove the wheat and keep it warm.

7. Measure the liquid in which the artichokes have been cooked. Add enough water to make 1 cup, or if there is over a cup, boil it down in a small pan until 1 cup remains.

8. Return the meat to the wok with the artichokes and keep warm.

9. Beat the egg yolks with a whisk or an electric mixer and gradually add the remaining lemon juice. Then add the cup of hot liquid in droplets, beating steadily. Pour the sauce into the wok and stir over low heat for about 1 minute, until the flavors permeate.

10. Serve with the steamed wheat, a crisp salad and dry red wine.

# RIBBONS OF VEAL WITH COGNAC, MUSHROOMS AND CREAM

Nicola Zanghi

4 servings

This dish is at its best when made with clarified butter. To clarify butter, melt the butter slowly and then let it settle. Skim off the fat and whey particles that have floated to the top and discard them. Pour the clear yellow liquid into a container and discard the milky substance on the bottom of the pan. I recommend clarifying large quantities as the butter can be refrigerated for one month.

2 TABLESPOONS MINCED
  SHALLOTS
½ CUP CLARIFIED BUTTER
1 CUP FINELY SLICED MUSHROOMS
1 CUP DRY WHITE WINE
1 CUP HEAVY CREAM
4 TABLESPOONS FLOUR
1½ POUNDS VEAL SCALOPPINE,
  CUT ¼-INCH THICK, EACH SLICE
  CUT INTO STRIPS ½-INCH WIDE

2 TABLESPOONS COGNAC OR
  GOOD BRANDY
½ TEASPOON SALT
FRESHLY GROUND PEPPER
NUTMEG
½ TEASPOON FRESH LEMON JUICE
2 TABLESPOONS BUTTER, AT ROOM
  TEMPERATURE

1. Over medium heat, sauté the shallots in ¼ cup of clarified butter until they are translucent. Add the mushrooms and stir until they are softened, about 3 minutes.

2. Turn up the heat and pour in the wine. Let it cook down to about ¼ of a cup. Pour in the cream and let it cook at a strong simmer for 5 minutes. Remove the sauce from the wok and set it aside.

3. Sprinkle the flour on the veal and mix well.

4. Wipe out the wok, turn the heat to high, and add the remaining butter. When it is hot, add the floured veal and stir-fry until it is brown on all sides.

5. Add the cognac carefully (it might catch fire). Stir, scraping down the sides of the wok with a wooden spoon.

6. Pour in the reserved sauce, lower the heat to medium and let it simmer for 2 minutes. While it is simmering, season with approximately ½ teaspoon salt, 7 to 8 grindings of pepper, a light dusting of freshly ground nutmeg and lemon juice.

7. Stir in the 2 tablespoons of butter, allowing it to melt into the sauce.

*Note:* I suggest serving this dish with a rice pilaf.

# Steamer Recipes

## STEAMED ARTICHOKES VINAIGRETTE

**Paul Rubinstein**

4 servings

**Steamed Artichokes:**
3 CLOVES GARLIC, CUT IN
  QUARTERS
½ CUP RED WINE VINEGAR
2 TABLESPOONS FRAGRANT OLIVE
  OIL (FRENCH OR ITALIAN)
10 CRUSHED BLACK PEPPERCORNS
1 TABLESPOON DRIED ROSEMARY
4 ARTICHOKES (MEDIUM-SIZED TO
  LARGE)
½ LEMON

2 TABLESPOONS WHITE VINEGAR
1 TEASPOON SALT
¼ TEASPOON FRESHLY GROUND
  BLACK PEPPER
1 TEASPOON FINELY MINCED
  ONION
1 HARD-COOKED EGG, RUBBED
  THROUGH A SIEVE
1 TABLESPOON FINELY MINCED
  PIMIENTO

**Vinaigrette:**
½ CUP OLIVE OIL

1. Put about 1 quart of water in the lower vessel of a steamer. Add to it the garlic cloves, vinegar, olive oil, peppercorns and rosemary. Turn on the heat and bring it to a boil.

2. While the water is heating, cut off the tops of the leaves of the artichokes and trim the bottoms so that they will sit upright. (One stroke of a sharp Chinese cleaver across the top and across the bottom is usually enough.) With a pair of shears, trim the remaining leaves to remove the sharp thorns. Rub all the cut surfaces with the lemon to prevent discoloration.

3. Place the artichokes in the steamer container above the water, cover and steam them for at least 30 minutes. Test for doneness by pulling out one leaf with a pair of tongs. It should come out with only a gentle tug. Otherwise steam 10 minutes longer and test again.

4. While the artichokes are steaming, prepare the vinaigrette by combining the olive oil, vinegar, salt, pepper, onion, egg and pimiento in a bowl. Mix well and serve the dressing in individual cups wtih the artichokes, which may be served either hot or chilled.

# RED BEANS COOKED WITH FESTIVAL RICE (SEKIHAN)

Toshio Morimoto

6 servings

This recipe requires advance planning, but it is quite easy to prepare.

1 CUP OF JAPANESE RED BEANS
  (*AZUKI* BEANS)*
1 POUND JAPANESE SWEET RICE
  (*MOCHI GOME*)*
1 TEASPOON BLACK SESAME
  SEEDS*
1 TEASPOON SALT
¼ TEASPOON MONOSODIUM
  GLUTAMATE (MSG) (OPTIONAL)

1. Place the beans in a colander or sieve and wash them under cold running water. Transfer them to a 2-quart pan, cover them with 8 cups of water and let them soak overnight. Bring them to a boil over high heat; reduce the heat to its lowest point and simmer the beans, uncovered, for 45 minutes, or until they are tender but still intact.

2. Drain the beans through a large sieve or colander set over a large mixing bowl. Reserve the bean liquid and cover the beans with cold water In another bowl. Cool to room temperature.

3. Stirring with a large spoon, wash the rice in a large pot or pan under cold running water until the draining water runs clear. Drain thoroughly and add the rice to the bowl of bean liquid. Soak for 8 hours or overnight, covered, in the refrigerator.

4. Drain the rice, discard the soaking liquid and combine the rice and the beans in a bowl and put it in an Oriental or other type of steamer.

5. In the bottom part of the steamer, bring the water to a boil over high heat; cover the steamer tightly, and steam for 40 minutes, replenishing the water in the pot if it boils away.

6. While the rice and beans are steaming, heat a small skillet over high heat until a drop of water flicked across its surface evaporates instantly. Add the sesame seeds and, shaking the pan gently, roast them for 2 to 3 minutes, until they are lightly toasted. Transfer the seeds to a small bowl and toss them with the salt and the MSG (if using it).

7. Sprinkle the seasoned sesame seeds (called *gomashio*) on top of the rice and serve.

    * These ingredients are available in Oriental grocery stores.

# STEAMED NEW POTATOES

Maurice Moore-Betty

3 to 4 servings

6 TO 8 SMALL NEW POTATOES
COARSE SALT
FINELY CHOPPED PARSLEY

1. If the potatoes are very new and freshly dug up, washing them under cold running water and scrubbing them with a hard brush is all that is necessary.

2. Put enough water in a pot to come up to the bottom of a steamer basket, strainer or colander. Arrange the potatoes in the steamer. Sprinkle them with a little coarse salt. Put the steamer over the water and cover it with a lid.

3. Bring the water to a boil and lower the heat so that the water simmers gently. Cover and steam the potatoes for about ½ hour; the time will depend on the age and size of the potatoes. A toothpick should pierce them easily.

4. Remove the lid for the last 5 minutes. Serve the potatoes sprinkled with chopped parsley. Steamed potatoes are a must with poached fish.


# STEAMED FISH STEAKS WITH EGG AND LEMON SAUCE

Florence Fabricant

4 servings

1 LARGE ONION, SLICED
1 LEMON, SLICED
2 LARGE SPRIGS FENNEL OR DILL
⅓ CUP CHOPPED FRESH FENNEL
  (OR ½ TEASPOON FENNEL OR
  ANISE SEEDS)
1 BAY LEAF
1 TEASPOON SALT
6 PEPPERCORNS

1½ CUPS WATER
2 POUNDS FISH STEAKS, ABOUT
  ¾-INCH THICK (TWO LARGE OR
  FOUR SMALL STEAKS—STRIPED
  BASS, COD, HALIBUT OR
  SALMON)
3 EGGS
2 TEASPOONS CORNSTARCH
JUICE OF 2 LEMONS

1. Spread the onion, lemon, one sprig of the fennel or dill, the chopped fennel or fennel seeds, the bay leaf, salt and peppercorns in the bottom of the steamer. Pour in the water, bring to a boil and boil uncovered for 5 minutes.

2. Place the fish steaks on a rack, set into the steamer, cover tightly and steam for 7 minutes.

3. Remove the fish to a platter, cover it with a towel wrung out in hot water and keep warm.

4. Strain the steaming liquid into a saucepan and bring it to a boil (there should be about 1 cup of liquid).

5. Beat the eggs. Mix the cornstarch and lemon juice and add it to the eggs and mix well. Transfer the mixture to a clean saucepan.

6. Add any liquid that has accumulated around the fish to the steaming liquid in the saucepan, and then slowly pour the hot fish liquid into the egg and lemon mixture, whisking constantly. Cook over low heat, whisking, until the sauce is thick and smooth; do not allow it to boil.

7. Pour the sauce over the fish, garnish it with the remaining sprig of fennel or dill and serve at once.

# STEAMED FISH WITH BUCKWHEAT NOODLES (SOBA MUSHI)

Toshio Morimoto

4 servings

12 OUNCES FILLET OF FLUKE
SALT
3 OUNCES DRIED BUCKWHEAT
NOODLES (*SOBA*)*
4 2-INCH SQUARE PIECES OF
KELP*
8 TEASPOONS SAKE

Sauce:
2 TABLESPOONS SOY SAUCE
2 TABLESPOONS SWEET SAKE
(*MIRIN*) OR SUBSTITUTE DRY
SHERRY

¾ CUP RECONSTITUTED DRIED
SOUP STOCK (*DASHI*)*
⅛ TEASPOON MONOSODIUM
GLUTAMATE (MSG) (OPTIONAL)

Garnish:
4 TEASPOONS FINELY GRATED
WHITE RADISH*
4 TEASPOONS FINELY GRATED
SCALLION

1. Cut the fluke fillet into four even pieces. Place a piece on a chopping board and butterfly it by making a lengthwise cut to within ½-inch of the far edge. Do the same with the other fillets. Salt them lightly.

2. Boil the buckheat noodles until half-cooked. Drain them, rinse with cold water and drain them again. Divide the noodles into four portions, and wrap a portion in each of the fillets.

3. In four individual serving bowls, place a piece of kelp. Arrange the rolled fluke on top, and pour about 2 teaspoons of sake over each fillet.

4. Arrange the bowls on a rack or steaming basket and place over boiling water. Steam them for 6 to 7 minutes.

5. While the fish steams, mix the soy sauce, sweet sake (or sherry), soup stock and MSG (if you are using it) in a small saucepan. Bring to a boil and pour over the fish before serving. Garnish the bowls with the radish and scallions.

* These ingredients are available in health food and Japanese food shops.

# STEAMED CARP

Raymond Sokolov

4 servings

1 1½-POUND CARP OR FLOUNDER,
   SCALED, CLEANED AND WITH
   THE HEAD LEFT ON
SALT
PEPPER
½ CUP OIL
JUICE OF 1 LEMON
1 BAY LEAF
4 SPRIGS PARSLEY
1 HANDFUL FRESH CORIANDER
   LEAVES (*CILANTRO* OR CHINESE
   PARSLEY)

1. Slash the fish in several places along the backbone.

2. Mix together the salt, pepper, oil, lemon juice, bay leaf and parsley sprigs in a shallow bowl. Put the fish in this marinade and let it sit at room temperature for 1 hour, turning it twice.

3. Prepare a steamer and bring the water to a boil.

4. Stuff the fish's cavity with the coriander leaves.

5. Set the bowl with the fish and the marinade in the steamer. Cover and steam for 20 minutes. Remove the bowl from the steamer and serve the fish immediately.


# STEAMED SEA BASS WITH SCALLIONS

Michael Tong

4 servings

1 2-POUND SEA BASS
1¼ TEASPOONS SALT
1 TEASPOON MONOSODIUM
   GLUTAMATE (MSG) (OPTIONAL)
2 TABLESPOONS WINE (RICE OR
   SHERRY)
4 SLICES OF GINGER, FINELY
   CHOPPED
6 SCALLIONS

¼ TEASPOON PEPPER
1 TEASPOON SESAME OIL
   (AVAILABLE IN ORIENTAL
   GROCERY STORES)
3 TABLESPOONS PEANUT OIL
2 TABLESPOONS CHICKEN STOCK
1 TABLESPOON SOY SAUCE
PARSLEY FOR GARNISHING THE
   PLATE

1. Clean the fish and rub it with the combined seasonings (1 teaspoon salt, ½ teaspoon MSG, if using it, 2 tablespoons wine and half of the chopped ginger).

2. Shred the scallions.

3. Place the fish in the steamer, steam over high heat for about 10 minutes and remove it. Sprinkle ¼ teaspoon black pepper and 1 teaspoon sesame oil over the fish.

4. Heat the peanut oil over high heat until it is smoking, then add the scallion and the remaining ginger shreds. Remove them from the oil and sprinkle over the fish.

5. Boil the chicken stock seasoned with the soy sauce, the remaining salt and MSG and pour it over the fish.

6. Garnish with parsley and serve.


# STEAMED FISH À LA RAIMONDO

Harvey Steiman

4 servings

4 WHOLE SMALL FISH (YELLOW-
   TAIL, SEA BASS, TROUT), ABOUT
   ¾ TO 1 POUND EACH
SALT
PEPPER
1 CUP WHITE WINE
1 TEASPOON DRIED ROSEMARY
1 CLOVE GARLIC, CRUSHED
1 TABLESPOON GRATED ONION
3 TABLESPOONS BUTTER, AT ROOM
   TEMPERATURE

1. Arrange the fish in a steamer basket and season them with salt and pepper.

2. Combine the wine, rosemary, garlic and onion in the steamer bottom. Bring them to a boil. Place the basket in the steamer and cover it. Steam 8 to 10 minutes, depending on the thickness of the fish.

3. Arrange the fish on a heated platter. Keep them warm.

4. Strain the steaming liquid into a skillet. Rapidly reduce the liquid by half. Swirl in the butter, taste for seasoning and spoon the sauce over the fish.

*Note:* If you don't have a steamer, you can use a large sauté pan with a lid. Crisscross celery ribs to make a platform for the fish, bring the wine and seasonings to a boil in the pan, place the fish on the bed of celery and cover to steam until done. Proceed as in the above recipe.

# STEAMED RED SNAPPER

Nathalie Dupree

4 to 6 servings

2 TO 2½ POUNDS RED SNAPPER
½ TEASPOON SALT
2 SCALLIONS
3 SLICES FRESH GINGER, CUT THE
    SIZE OF QUARTERS
¼ CUP LIGHT SOY SAUCE
2 TABLESPOONS SESAME SEED
    OIL (AVAILABLE IN HEALTH FOOD
    AND ORIENTAL GROCERY
    STORES)

1. Clean the fish, sprinkle it with salt and place it in a wide, shallow dish with a rim about 1-inch high.

2. Place the dish on a rack in a wok or frying pan and fill the bottom of the vessel with water. Cover it and steam the fish for 20 minutes.

3. While the fish is steaming, shred the scallions lengthwise and cut them into 1-inch lengths. Sliver the ginger.

4. Pour the liquid from the fish dish into a pan with the soy sauce and sesame oil and heat the liquids.

5. Spread the scallion shreds and ginger strips over the fish and pour the soy sauce mixture over the fish. Serve at once.


# STEAMED NORTHERN PIKE
# WITH HERB BUTTER

Ruth Ellen Church

6 servings

This is a simple, "pure" way to cook very fresh fish to keep its fine flavor. Unsalted butter might be used in keeping with a low salt diet. Permitting diners to sauce the fish as they wish favors other kinds of diets.

1 3-POUND NORTHERN PIKE OR
    LAKE TROUT
LEAVES FROM A BUNCH OF
    CELERY
6 PARSLEY SPRIGS
2 SMALL ONIONS OR 3 TO 4
    SHALLOTS, COARSELY CHOPPED
1 CUP (2 STICKS) MELTED BUTTER

1 TABLESPOON MINCED CHIVES
    OR SCALLION
1 TABLESPOON MINCED FRESH
    PARSLEY
1 TABLESPOON MINCED
    WATERCRESS
¼ CUP DRY WHITE WINE
¼ CUP LEMON JUICE

1. Clean the fish, leaving on the head and tail. Fill the fish with the celery leaves, parsley sprigs and the onions or shallots.

2. Place the fish on the dish in which it will be served and place the dish on a rack or in a steaming basket. The rack should be about 2 inches above the boiling water in a wok, poacher or roaster. Cover the pot and steam the fish approximately 10 minutes to the pound. Do not overcook the fish. Test with a fork—when the flesh is flaky, the fish is cooked.

3. While the fish cooks, combine the remaining ingredients and warm them in a saucepan. Pass the sauce separately.

# STEAMED FILLET OF SOLE
# WITH FERMENTED BLACK BEANS

Grace Zia Chu

4 servings

4 SOLE FILLETS, TOTALING 1
  POUND
2 TABLESPOONS SHREDDED FRESH
  GINGER ROOT
2 STALKS SCALLION, CUT IN
  2-INCH PIECES
1 TABLESPOON FERMENTED BLACK
  BEANS*
½ TABLESPOON VEGETABLE OIL
1 TABLESPOON DRY SHERRY
1 TABLESPOON SOY SAUCE

1. Rinse and pat the sole dry with paper towels. Lay the fillets flat on a plate with a raised rim, to hold the liquid that will accumulate.

2. Add the ginger shreds, scallion and fermented black beans. Pour the oil, sherry and soy sauce over the fillets.

3. In a saucepan large enough to hold the plate, place a rack or steamer that stands about 2 inches above the bottom. Add 1 inch of water. Bring the water to a boil, then put the plate of fish on the rack. Cover the saucepan and steam the fish for 10 minutes over high heat. There will be about ¼ cup of liquid (from the condensed steam) in the plate. Sauce the fish with it and serve it hot.

* Fermented black beans can be bought from Chinese grocery stores. They keep well for months in a tightly-closed jar.

# STEAMED FISH WITH BEAN CURD, HERBS AND LEMON

**Elizabeth Colchie**

2 servings

½ POUND WHITE-FLESHED FISH
  FILLETS, CUT INTO LARGE
  SERVING PIECES
2 CAKES SOFT BEAN CURD
  (ABOUT ¾ POUND), CUT INTO
  DICE
1 TEASPOON SALT
2 TABLESPOONS FINELY SNIPPED
  CHIVES

1 TABLESPOON FINELY MINCED
  CORIANDER LEAVES (*CILANTRO*
  OR CHINESE PARSLEY)
2 TABLESPOONS MINCED PARSLEY
2 TABLESPOONS DRY SHERRY
2 TABLESPOONS LEMON JUICE
WHITE PEPPER
LEMON SLICES FOR GARNISH

1. In a heatproof serving dish, arrange the fish and bean curd. Evenly sprinkle them with the salt, chives, coriander leaves, parsley, sherry, lemon juice and pepper to taste.

2. Place the fish on the steaming rack over boiling water, cover, and steam for 8 to 10 minutes, or until the fish flakes easily. Garnish with slices of lemon.

# PORK WON TON APPETIZERS

**Jane Moulton**

5 to 6 dozen pieces

3 MEDIUM-SIZED DRIED CHINESE
  MUSHROOMS*
1 CAN (ABOUT 8 OUNCES) WATER
  CHESTNUTS, DRAINED AND
  CHOPPED
2 POUNDS LEAN GROUND PORK
¾ CUP CHOPPED SCALLIONS
  (INCLUDING GREEN TOPS)
3 TABLESPOONS CORNSTARCH

2 TABLESPOONS SOY SAUCE
1½ TEASPOONS SALT
2 TEASPOONS SESAME OIL*
1 EGG, LIGHTLY BEATEN
¾ TO 1 POUND WON TON NOODLE
  SKINS* (ABOUT ¾-INCH SQUARE)
1 EGG, LIGHTLY BEATEN

1. Soak the dried mushrooms in water for 30 minutes. Drain them, discard the tough stems and cut the mushrooms into small pieces. In a large bowl, combine the mushroom pieces with all the remaining ingredients except the noodle skins and the egg. Mix well.

2. Oil plates that are slightly smaller than your steamer baskets so that steam can enter from below and circulate. Sesame oil is good for this.

3. Using a pastry brush, brush all but the outer edges of the noodle skins with the egg. Place the skins on a circle made with your left thumb and first finger (if you're right-handed). Place a rounded tablespoon of meat mixture in the center, pressing down to form a pouch. Squeeze the top to close it, but leave a little of the meat exposed.

4. As you make each one, place it on an oiled plate. Don't crowd the plates; the steam must circulate. Place in a covered steamer and steam about 20 minutes, or until the noodles are translucent and no longer taste raw. Unless you used too much pork filling in each, the meat will also be done when the noodles are cooked. Serve them hot as an appetizer.

*Note:* These are also good as an extra dish for the main course of a Chinese meal. They can be frozen before steaming, if desired. Leftovers can also be frozen and reheated, but with some loss of quality.

\* These ingredients are available in Oriental grocery stores.

## STEAMED CHICKEN AND HAM LOAF
## WITH CREAM SAUCE

Elizabeth Colchie

2 to 3 servings

1 POUND CHICKEN BREAST
(WHOLE, WITH BONE)
1 EGG WHITE
4 TABLESPOONS DRY SHERRY
3 TEASPOONS CORNSTARCH
½ TEASPOON SALT
½ TEASPOON SUGAR
BIG PINCH WHITE PEPPER

½ CUP LOOSELY-PACKED WATER
CHESTNUTS, FINELY MINCED
1 CUP (4 OUNCES) FINELY MINCED
BAKED HAM
3 TABLESPOONS MINCED CHIVES
2 TEASPOONS MINCED DILL
⅓ CUP HEAVY CREAM

1. Skin and bone the chicken breast and blend the meat (there should be about 8 ounces) in the food processor until it is a paste.

2. Combine the egg white, 2 tablespoons of sherry, 2 teaspoons cornstarch, the sugar, salt and pepper in a cup and add to the processor. Blend briefly and turn into a mixing bowl with the water chestnuts, ham, 2 tablespoons of chives and dill and mix very well.

3. Oil a baking-serving dish that will fit into the steamer and with wet hands mound the chicken neatly in the center forming a circle about 5 inches in diameter. Steam it over moderate heat for 20 minutes. Pour the accumulated broth into a small pan; add the cream and the remaining (1 tablespoon) chives. In a cup, mix the remaining teaspoon of cornstarch with the remaining sherry and add them to the liquid. Simmer the sauce, stirring, until it thickens. Season to taste.

5. Cut the loaf of meat into about 10 slices and arrange them, overlapping, in the serving dish. Pour the sauce over the top and steam for 10 minutes longer.

# CHINESE PORK DUMPLINGS (DIM SUM)

Michael Tong

30 pieces

1 POUND GROUND PORK
½ CUP CHOPPED BAMBOO SHOOTS
2 TEASPOONS SOY SAUCE
½ TEASPOON SALT
2 TEASPOONS CORNSTARCH
2 TEASPOONS SESAME OIL*
¼ TEASPOON BLACK PEPPER
½ CUP SOAKED AND CHOPPED
　CHINESE MUSHROOMS*
2 TEASPOONS DRY SHERRY
1 EGG
30 PIECES *DIM SUM* SKINS*

1. Put the ground pork, chopped bamboo shoots, soy sauce, salt, cornstarch, sesame oil, black pepper, chopped Chinese mushrooms and the sherry in a large mixing bowl. Blend them very rigorously and thoroughly with your hands and fingers.

2. Beat the egg in a bowl.

3. Place a piece of *dim sum* skin in your palm. Wet the upper side of the skin with the egg. Place about 1 tablespoon of filling on the center of the wetted skin, then pinch up the sides to the center.

4. Place the dumplings on a damp cloth in a bamboo steamer and steam over high heat for about 15 minutes. Check to see that the pork is cooked. Steam a bit longer if necessary.

　* These ingredients are available in Oriental grocery stores.


# STEAMED LEMON-ORANGE SPONGE CAKE

Elizabeth Colchie

5 EXTRA LARGE EGGS, AT ROOM
　TEMPERATURE
1 TABLESPOON ORANGE JUICE
1 CUP SUGAR
⅛ TEASPOON SALT
1 TEASPOON GRATED LEMON RIND
½ TEASPOON GRATED ORANGE
　RIND
¼ TEASPOON ALMOND EXTRACT
¾ CUP ALL-PURPOSE FLOUR
¼ CUP CORNSTARCH
1½ TABLESPOONS MELTED BUTTER

1. In a bowl of an electric mixer, beat the eggs, orange juice, sugar and salt at high speed until very thick and pale, about 15 minutes; beat in the grated rinds and almond extract.

2. Place the flour and cornstarch in a sifter and gradually sift it into the egg mixture, folding gently with a spatula to incorporate the dry ingredients into the eggs without deflating them; fold in the butter.

3. Fit a circle of parchment into the bottom of a 9-inch circular cake pan and pour in the batter. It will come to the top of the pan, but it will not rise during the baking-steaming process.

4. Place the pan on the steamer rack over rapidly boiling water and cover tightly. Steam over moderate heat for 25 minutes. Remove the cake and let it cool for 10 minutes. Run a knife around the edge and invert it onto a serving dish.

5. Serve the cake warm with fresh fruit sauce, such as raspberry, strawberry or peach. Or fold together sour cream and finely minced preserved kumquats as a sauce.

# PEARL BALLS

Gloria Bley Miller

20 dumplings

½ CUP GLUTINOUS RICE (AVAILABLE IN ORIENTAL GROCERIES)
1 POUND PORK (BONELESS BUTT OR LOIN)
1 SCALLION
2 SLICES FRESH GINGER ROOT
4 WATER CHESTNUTS

1 EGG
1 TABLESPOON SOY SAUCE
1 TEASPOON CORNSTARCH
2 TEASPOONS MEDIUM-DRY SHERRY
½ TEASPOON SUGAR
½ TEASPOON SALT

1. Rinse the rice to remove some of its surface starch and place it in a bowl. Soak it for 4 hours in cold water to cover. Drain the rice and spread it out on a towel to dry.

2. Mince or grind the pork, including some of its fat, and place it in a bowl. Mince the scallion, ginger root and water chestnuts. Add them to the meat.

3. Beat the egg lightly. Add it to the mixture, along with the soy sauce, cornstarch, sherry, sugar and salt. Blend well by hand, but do not overwork the mixture.

4. Form the pork and seasonings into walnut-sized balls, moistening the hands from time to time to keep the mixture from adhering. Roll each ball in the rice to coat it completely.

5. Line the trays of a Chinese bamboo steamer with a double thickness of dampened cheesecloth. Arrange the pearl balls on these so they're about ½ inch apart (to allow for expansion). Steam them over boiling water until they are done, about 40 minutes. Serve the pearl balls hot.

# JAPANESE STEAMED CHICKEN AND MUSHROOM SOUP (KABURA MUSHI)

Toshio Morimoto

4 servings

1 TEASPOON GREEN HORSERADISH POWDER (*WASABI*)*
4 SMALL MUSHROOMS, CUT IN HALF
4 MEDIUM-SIZED SHRIMP, PEELED AND DEVEINED
⅛ TEASPOON SALT
¼ TEASPOON MONOSODIUM GLUTAMATE (MSG) (OPTIONAL)
4 OUNCES (¼ POUND) BONED CHICKEN, CUT INTO 16 PIECES

4¼ TEASPOONS SOY SAUCE
12 GINGKO NUTS (*GINNAN*)*
3 WHITE TURNIPS (2 OUNCES EACH), PEELED AND FINELY GRATED
1 EGG YOLK
2 CUPS RECONSTITUTED SOUP STOCK (*DASHI*)*
4 TEASPOONS SAKE
4 TEASPOONS CORNSTARCH MIXED WITH 2 TABLESPOONS WATER

1. Mix the horseradish powder with a few drops of water to make a paste and set it aside for at least 15 minutes to let the flavor develop.

2. Sprinkle the mushrooms and shrimp with the salt and half the MSG (if you are using it). Sprinkle the chicken bits with ¼ teaspoon of soy sauce.

3. On each of four small heatproof plates, arrange the mushrooms, shrimp, chicken and gingko nuts, divided evenly.

4. In a small dish, combine the grated turnip with the egg yolk and spoon a mound onto each plate. Arrange the plates in a steaming basket or on a rack; place them over water and steam them for 7 minutes after the water has come to a boil.

5. While the food is steaming, bring the soup stock to a boil. Add the remaining soy sauce and MSG (if using), the sake and the cornstarch mixture. Stir constantly until the soup thickens and clears.

6. Slide the steamed food into four soup bowls, and pour the soup into each of them. Garnish each with a dab of green horseradish.

* These ingredients are available in Japanese food stores.

# STEAMED EGGS WITH SHRIMP

Gloria Bley Miller

4 servings

½ CUP RAW SHRIMP
2 SCALLIONS
2 TEASPOONS MEDIUM-DRY SHERRY
½ TEASPOON SOY SAUCE
2 TEASPOONS PEANUT OIL
FEW DROPS CHINESE SESAME OIL
    (AVAILABLE IN HEALTH FOOD
    AND ORIENTAL GROCERY
    STORES)
4 EGGS
1 CUP CHICKEN STOCK

1. Mince the shrimp and scallions and combine them in a bowl with the sherry, ¼ teaspoon soy sauce, 1 teaspoon of the peanut oil and the sesame oil. Toss well to blend. Let the mixture stand for 15 minutes, turning occasionally.

2. Beat the eggs very gently, only enough to blend the yolks and whites.

3. Heat the chicken stock until it is hot, but not boiling.

4. Add the shrimp mixture to the eggs, then add the hot stock in a trickle, stirring it in slowly.

5. Lightly brush a 10-inch glass pie pan or similar heatproof dish with the remaining peanut oil and pour in the egg mixture.

6. Put water to a depth of 2 to 3 inches in the bottom of a steamer and bring it to a boil, then put a rack or basket in the pot, tall enough to keep the dish out of the water. Add the dish with the egg mixture.

7. Cover and let the egg mixture steam over medium heat until it is custard-like, about 30 minutes. Check for doneness with a toothpick; it should emerge clean.

8. Sprinkle the eggs lightly with the remaining soy sauce and serve.

# Fire Pot Recipes

## CHINESE CHRYSANTHEMUM FIRE POT I

Grace Zia Chu

6 servings

Chrysanthemum Fire Pot is enjoyed in the winter in homes and restaurants all over China. This is a typical variation from the eastern parts of China, including Shanghai, Hangchow and Nanking. The name, Chrysanthemum Fire Pot is used even if no fresh chrysanthemum petals are available. If you use a copper pot with a "cage" for the liquid alcohol, the flames shooting out will be vari-colored and give the illusion of a flower. Each diner dips his food into the communal pot to cook, using either chopsticks or a small wire basket.

24 UNCOOKED SHRIMPS
1 LARGE CHICKEN BREAST
1 POUND FILLET OF SOLE
8 CHICKEN LIVERS
18 CHERRYSTONE CLAMS
12 RAW OYSTERS
4 OUNCES CELLOPHANE NOODLES
4 SQUARES OF BEAN CURD
½ POUND FRESH SPINACH

½ POUND CHINESE CELERY
   CABBAGE
1 LARGE WHITE CHRYSANTHEMUM
1 CUP SOY SAUCE
½ CUP RED WINE VINEGAR
¼ CUP SUGAR
6 MEDIUM-SIZED EGGS
3 QUARTS CHICKEN BROTH

1. Shell and devein the shrimps. Split them lengthwise, but do not cut all the way through.

2. Skin and bone the chicken breast. With a cleaver, cut the chicken into thin strips, on the bias.

3. Slice the fillet of sole into strips, comparable to the chicken.

4. Cut each of the chicken livers into four pieces.

5. Open the clams and oysters and arrange all of the fish and meat on six 10-inch plates and chill until you are ready to serve.

6. Soak the cellophane noodles in very hot water for 10 minutes. Drain them and cut into 3-inch lengths for easier handling. Put them in a serving bowl.

7. Cut each piece of bean curd into eight equal pieces and put it in a bowl.

8. Wash and trim the spinach and cabbage and cut the cabbage into 2-inch pieces. Put them into separate serving bowls.

9. Wash the chrysanthemum and put it on a serving plate.

10. Combine the soy sauce, wine vinegar and sugar and pour it into six small bowls and place them around the table for dipping.

11. Break each of the eggs into individual cups and distribute them around the table.

12. If a traditional Chrysanthemum pot is to be used, put it on an asbestos mat and set it in the middle of the table. Add boiling chicken broth to the trough of the pot and make sure it simmers throughout the meal.

13. The guests should pull off a chrysanthemum petal or two to cook with any of the foods they choose.

14. When most of the fish and meat have been eaten, add all the vegetables to the pot, cover it, and cook them for a minute. Continue feasting.

15. Lastly, each guest poaches an egg in the wonderfully flavored broth and removes it to his dipping bowl, along with some of the broth.

# CHINESE CHRYSANTHEMUM FIRE POT II

Michael Tong

6 servings

Use a regular Chinese fire pot if you have one. Use charcoal as a source of heat (see introduction), or substitute Sterno. An electric skillet may be used for this dish, or a basin of some sort set on a heating unit that will assure continuous boiling as the food is cooked. A fondue dish could conceivably be used, but for no more than one or two people. Provide each guest with chopsticks or a fondue fork and a bowl of dipping sauce, or let the guests mix their own from the various ingredients. The ingredients given are approximate; add more for additional guests. No more than four to six people can comfortably use one fire pot.

½ POUND PER SERVING OF LAMB, BEEF, CHICKEN, FISH, SHRIMP OR A COMBINATION: IF SHRIMP IS USED, SPRINKLE EACH POUND OF CLEAN, DE-VEINED SHRIMP WITH 1 TEASPOON OF CORNSTARCH AND 2 TABLESPOONS OF DRY SHERRY AND LET STAND FOR AN HOUR BEFORE SERVING

BEAN CURD
CABBAGE
SPINACH
WATERCRESS
MUSHROOMS
CELLOPHANE NOODLES
ONION SLICES

1. Arrange thinly sliced lamb, beef, breast of chicken, sea bass or other fish, or any combination of these ingredients, on chilled plates. Keep chilled until ready to serve. Count on about ½ pound of meat or fish per person. Meat, fish, or a combination of the two are generally cooked and eaten first, then the vegetables and so on.

2. Add a quart or more of boiling water to the fire pot basin, electric skillet or whatever, depending on the size of the utensil and the number of guests to be served. Keep it boiling throughout the meal.

*Continued from preceding page*

3. Supplement these with a combination of various ingredients; bean curd cut into thick strips, coarsely cut Chinese cabbage, coarsely cut spinach, watercress, thinly sliced mushrooms, cellophane noodles soaked in boiling water until wilted, onion slices and any other suitable vegetables.

4. Let each guest serve himself by picking up various ingredients with chopsticks or spearing them with forks. Guests dip one morsel at a time into the boiling liquid and cook it to the desired degree of doneness. As each bite is cooked, it is dipped quickly into the sauce and eaten immediately while hot.

5. When all the food has been cooked and eaten, the remaining broth is ladled into the individual sauce bowls and drunk.

**Dipping Sauce:**

SESAME PASTE* OR SUBSTITUTE
  PEANUT BUTTER
CHOPPED SCALLIONS
CHOPPED FRESH CORIANDER
  (*CILANTRO* OR CHINESE
  PARSLEY)*
SOY SAUCE, PREFERABLY DARK
WHITE VINEGAR

DRY SHERRY
MONOSODIUM GLUTAMATE (MSG)
  (OPTIONAL)
CHILI PEPPER WITH GARLIC* OR
  FINELY CHOPPED GARLIC MIXED
  WITH HOT PEPPER SAUCE
SHRIMP ROE SOY SAUCE (*LOW
  CHI*)*

For each person, mix 2 teaspoons of sesame paste, 1 tablespoon each of scallions, coriander and soy sauce, 1½ teaspoons of vinegar, 1 tablespoon of sherry, ⅛ teaspoon of MSG (if using), ¼ teaspoon of chili with garlic, and 1 teaspoon of shrimp roe sauce in a bowl. There should be about ⅓ cup of sauce in each bowl.

* These ingredients are available in Oriental grocery stores.

---

## JAPANESE FIRE POT (SHABU SHABU)

Toshio Morimoto

4 servings

**Dipping Sauce:**
4 TABLESPOONS WHITE SESAME
  SEEDS, TOASTED AND GROUND
  INTO A PASTE
3 TABLESPOONS SAKE
2 TABLESPOONS SOY SAUCE
½ CUP DRIED AND RECONSTI-
  TUTED SOUP STOCK (*DASHI*)*
PINCH MONOSODIUM GLUTAMATE
  (MSG) (OPTIONAL)

1. To make the dipping sauce, heat a small frying pan over high heat until a drop of water flicked across its surface evaporates instantly. Add the sesame seeds and, shaking the pan almost continuously, warm them until they are a

pale gold and their aroma is released; grind them to a paste with mortar and pestle or, more easily, pulverize them at high speed in an electric blender.

2. Over high heat, heat the sake to lukewarm. Remove the pan from the heat and ignite the sake with a kitchen match, shaking the pan gently until the flame dies out. Pour the sake into a small bowl and cool it to room temperature.

3. Place the sesame paste in the mortar or electric blender, add the flamed sake, soy sauce, soup stock and the optional MSG. Mix or blend. To serve, pour into individual serving bowls.

**Fire Pot:**

8 CARROTS, SCRAPED AND CUT LENGTHWISE INTO STRIPS ¼-INCH WIDE BY 2 INCHES LONG
1 POUND BONELESS SHELL OR SIRLOIN STEAK, SLICED IN STRIPS ⅛-INCH THICK BY 3 INCHES LONG
1 POUND CHINESE CABBAGE, TRIMMED AT THE BASE, LEAVES SEPARATED AND CUT CROSSWISE INTO 2-INCH STRIPS
12 YOUNG SPINACH LEAVES, STRIPPED FROM THEIR STEMS
2 CAKES SOY BEAN CURD (TOFU),* FRESH, CANNED OR INSTANT, CUT INTO 1-INCH CUBES
8 SMALL WHITE MUSHROOMS
1 4-INCH SQUARE DRIED KELP (KOMBU)* (OPTIONAL)
6 CUPS CHICKEN BROTH OR WATER OR COMBINATION OF THE TWO

1. Bring 1 cup of water to a boil in a small saucepan. Drop in the carrot strips. Return to the boil, then drain and cool them.

2. Arrange the beef, vegetables and all other materials on a large serving platter. Chill them until you are ready to serve.

3. To serve, use a Mongolian fire pot; hot pot; heavy, shallow casserole; electric skillet; or heatproof earthenware pot. Pour the broth or water into the pot of your choice and add the kelp (kombu), if you are using it. Bring to a boil, then adjust the heat so that the liquid simmers throughout the meal. Each guest selects pieces of food from the platter and dips them into the simmering broth. Cook the vegetables until they are done. Swish the beef about in the simmering broth or water until it is cooked to taste. Dip the cooked food into the sauce. When all of the meat and accompaniments have been eaten, ladle the broth into the dipping bowl and finish the main course with soup!

* These ingredients are available in health food and Japanese food shops.

# MONGOLIAN FIRE POT
# WITH SESAME SEED BUNS

**Florence Lin**

14 2½-inch buns

Sesame seed buns traditionally accompany Mongolian fire pots. However, they are also excellent with other dishes and with soups. If you make them in advance, they can be wrapped in foil and reheated in a 350 F. oven for 15 minutes.

**To Make the Buns:**
1 TEASPOON ACTIVE DRY YEAST
1 CUP LUKEWARM WATER
2 TEASPOONS SUGAR
3 CUPS ALL-PURPOSE FLOUR
3 TABLESPOONS PEANUT BUTTER
2 TEASPOONS SESAME OIL
1 TEASPOON SALT
1 TABLESPOON CORN SYRUP
   COMBINED WITH 2 TABLESPOONS
   WARM WATER
½ CUP WHITE SESAME SEEDS

1. Dissolve the yeast in the lukewarm water for 2 minutes. Add the sugar, mix, and let it stand for 2 more minutes.

2. Put the flour in a large mixing bowl. Add the dissolved yeast to the flour. Knead it and gather it into a ball. Add more water, a little at a time, if the dough seems too dry. The dough should be pliable, soft, and smooth. Cover with a damp cloth and let it rise in a warm place for about 30 minutes.

3. Mix the peanut butter with the sesame oil and set it aside.

4. Knead the dough on a lightly floured surface for 5 minutes, sprinkling the dough with a little flour from time to time while kneading.

5. Roll the dough out into a large rectangular sheet about ¼-inch thick, 20 inches long, and 8 inches wide. Sprinkle the salt on it and spread the peanut butter mixture evenly over the dough. Roll the dough as a jelly roll, lengthwise, to make a 1-inch-diameter cylinder and cut it into 1½-inch-long sections. You should have about 14 pieces. Seal each section at both ends by pulling and pinching toward the center. With your hands, shape the dough into a 3-inch-diameter round, ½-inch-thick bun.

6. Brush the top of each bun with the diluted corn syrup and dip the top into the sesame seeds. Use a rolling pin to lightly press in the seeds.

7. Place the buns, sesame-side-up, in 2 large skillets. Cover and let them rest for 20 minutes. Put the skillets on the burners and turn the heat to medium-low. Let the buns cook for about 10 minutes, shaking the pans occasionally. Turn over the buns, cover, and brown the sesame seed sides for 10 minutes. Serve them hot.

**Ingredients for the Fire Pot:**

For easy slicing, have the butcher remove the lamb bone, tendons and gristle. Tie the meat with strings as for a roast. Freeze it until it is firm enough to cut with an electric slicer or cleaver.

3 POUNDS PARTIALLY FROZEN LEG OF LAMB, WITH BONES, TENDONS, AND GRISTLE REMOVED

2 OUNCES CELLOPHANE NOODLES, SOAKED IN BOILING WATER FOR 20 MINUTES, THEN DRAINED AND CUT INTO 4-INCH-LONG PIECES

½ POUND FRESH SPINACH (TENDER PARTS ONLY), WELL WASHED

½ POUND CELERY CABBAGE, CUT INTO 2-BY-1-INCH PIECES

1 TABLESPOON RED FERMENTED BEAN CURD*

6 TO 8 CUPS LAMB BROTH, MADE FROM SCRAPS AND BONE FROM THE LEG OF LAMB

Sauce:

2 TABLESPOONS SESAME PASTE, DILUTED WITH 4 TABLESPOONS WARM WATER

¼ CUP LIGHT SOY SAUCE

2 TABLESPOONS SESAME OIL

2 TABLESPOONS WINE VINEGAR

1 TABLESPOON SUGAR

2 TEASPOONS CHINESE HOT PEPPER OIL*

1 SCALLION, FINELY CHOPPED

1 TEASPOON FINELY MINCED GARLIC

1 TEASPOON FRESH GINGER JUICE (USE A GARLIC PRESS)

¼ CUP FINELY CHOPPED CORIANDER LEAVES* (*CILANTRO* OR CHINESE PARSLEY)

¼ CUP WATER

1. Slice the meat into 2-by-4-by-⅛-inch-thick pieces and arrange it in one layer, with pieces partly overlapping, on six plates.

2. Put the soaked cellophane noodles, spinach, celery cabbage, and bean curd in two serving bowls.

3. Pour the broth into either a traditional fire pot or an electric casserole or skillet on the dining table. Bring the broth to a boil. The broth must continue to simmer during the time the dish is served and eaten.

4. In a bowl, mix the sauce ingredients well. Place 2 to 3 tablespoons mixed sauce in each of six individual rice bowls.

5. Put the lamb pieces, vegetables and buns on the table and allow each guest to serve himself, holding chopsticks in one hand and the sauce bowl in the other.

6. The method of cooking is for each person to use the chopsticks to dip a thin slice of lamb into the boiling broth and let the lamb cook to the desired degree. The cooked meat is then dipped into one's own sauce bowl and eaten while hot. Serve the sesame seed buns during the meal. After all the lamb has been eaten, drop the vegetables, noodles, and bean curd into the broth, cook briefly, and eat it while it is hot. This ends the meal with a tasty hot soup with vegetables.

*Note:* It is more comfortable if not more than six persons share a pot at one table.

---

* These ingredients are available in Oriental grocery stores.

# EDITORS

Arnold Goldman
Barbara Spiegel
Lyn Stallworth

# EDITORIAL ASSISTANT

Christopher Carter

# EDITORIAL CONSULTANTS

Wendy Afton Rieder
Kate Slate

# CONTRIBUTORS

## Introduction by Lyn Stallworth

**Michael Batterberry,** author of several books on food, art and social history, is also a painter, and is editor and food critic for a number of national magazines. He has taught at James Beard's cooking classes in New York and many of his original recipes have appeared in *House & Garden, House Beautiful* and *Harper's Bazaar.*

**Paula J. Buchholz** is the regional co-ordinator for the National Culinary Apprenticeship Program. She has been a food writer for the *Detroit Free Press* and for the *San Francisco Examiner.*

**Vilma Liacouras Chantiles,** author of *The Food of Greece,* writes a food and consumer column for the *Scarsdale* (New York) *Inquirer* and a monthly food column for the *Athenian Magazine* (Athens, Greece).

**Grace Zia Chu,** author of the extraordinarily successful *The Pleasures of Chinese Cooking* and more recently, *Madame Chu's Chinese Cooking School,* has taught Chinese cooking both in her own school and at the China Institute of America in New York City.

**Ruth Ellen Church,** a syndicated wine columnist for the *Chicago Tribune,* had been food editor for that newspaper for more than thirty years when she recently retired. The author of seven cookbooks, her most recent book is *Entertaining with Wine.* Mrs. Church's *Wines and Cheeses of the Midwest* will be published in the fall of 1977.

**Elizabeth Colchie** is a noted food consultant who has done extensive recipe development and testing as well as research into the history of foods and cookery. She was on the editorial staff of *The Cooks' Catalogue* and has written numerous articles for such magazines as *Gourmet, House & Garden* and *Family Circle*.

**Carol Cutler,** who has been a food columnist for the *Washington Post,* is a graduate of the Cordon Bleu and L'École des Trois Gourmands in Paris. She is the author of *Haute Cuisine for Your Heart's Delight* and *The Six-Minute Soufflé and Other Culinary Delights.* She has also written for *House & Garden, American Home* and *Harper's Bazaar.*

**Julie Dannenbaum** is the founding director of the largest non-professional cooking school in the country, the Creative Cooking School in Philadelphia. She is the author of *Julie Dannenbaum's Creative Cooking School* and *Menus for All Occasions.* She is also Director of the Gritti Palace Hotel Cooking School in Venice and The Grand Hotel Cooking School in Rome.

**Nathalie Dupree** has been Director of Rich's Cooking School in Atlanta, Georgia, since it opened in September, 1975. She has an Advanced Certificate from the London Cordon Bleu and has owned restaurants in Spain and Georgia.

**Florence Fabricant** is a free-lance writer, reporting on restaurants and food for *The New York Times, New York* magazine and other publications. She was on the staff of *The Cooks' Catalogue* and editor of the paperback edition.

**Emanuel and Madeline Greenberg** co-authored *Whiskey in the Kitchen* and are consultants to the food and beverage industry. Emanuel, a home economist, is a regular contributor to the food columns of *Playboy* magazine.

**Carole Lalli** is a contributing editor to *New West* magazine and its restaurant reviewer. She formerly ran a catering business in New York.

**Jeanne Lesem,** Family Editor of United Press International, is the author of *The Pleasures of Preserving and Pickling.*

**Florence Lin** has been teaching Chinese cooking at the China Institute in New York for 17 years. She is the author of *Florence Lin's Chinese Regional Cookbook* and *Florence Lin's Chinese Vegetarian Cookbook* and was the chief food consultant for the *Cooking of China* in Time-Life Books' *Foods of the World* series.

**Gloria Bley Miller** is the author of *Learn Chinese Cooking in Your Own Kitchen* and *The Thousand Recipe Chinese Cookbook.*

**Maurice Moore-Betty,** owner-operator of The Civilized Art Cooking School, food consultant and restaurateur, is author of *Cooking for Occasions, The Maurice Moore-Betty Cooking School Book of Fine Cooking* and *The Civilized Art of Salad Making.*

**Toshio Morimoto** is the owner of Kitcho, a highly regarded Japanese restaurant in New York City. He was the consulting chef for *Cooking of Japan* in Time-Life Books' *Foods of the World* series.

**Jane Moulton,** a food writer for the *Plain Dealer* in Cleveland, took her degree in foods and nutrition. As well as reporting on culinary matters and reviewing food-related books for the *Plain Dealer,* she has worked in recipe development, public relations and catering.

**Paul Rubinstein** is the author of *Feasts for Two, The Night Before Cookbook* and *Feasts for Twelve (or More).* He is a stockbroker and the son of pianist Artur Rubinstein.

**Raymond Sokolov,** author of *The Saucier's Apprentice,* is a free-lance writer with a particular interest in food.

**Harvey Steiman** is food editor of the *Miami Herald.* He has taught cooking classes and lectured on wine and restaurants at the Food and Hotel School of Florida International University.

**Michael Tong** is Managing Director of three of the finest Chinese restaurants in New York: Shun Lee Dynasty, Shun Lee Palace and Hunam.

**Joanne Will** is food editor of the *Chicago Tribune* and a member of three Chicago wine and food societies.

**Nicola Zanghi** is the owner-chef of Restaurant Zanghi in Glen Cove, New York. He started his apprenticeship under his father at the age of thirteen, and is a graduate of two culinary colleges. He is an instructor at the Cordon Bleu school in New York City.